FROMMER'S
WALKING TOURS
NEW YORK

BY
RENA BULKIN

PRENTICE HALL TRAVEL

NEW YORK • LONDON • TORONTO • SYDNEY
TOKYO • SINGAPORE

FROMMER BOOKS

Published by Prentice Hall General Reference
A division of Simon & Schuster Inc.
15 Columbus Circle
New York, NY 10023

Library of Congress Cataloging-in-Publication Data
Bulkin, Rena.
Frommer's Walking Tours: New York/by Rena Bulkin.
    p. cm.
Includes index.
ISBN 0-671-79762-X
1. New York (N.Y.)—Tours. 2. Walking—New York (N.Y.)—Guidebooks.
3. Historic sites—New York (N.Y.)—Guidebooks. I. Title.
F128.18.B84   1993
917.47′10443—dc20   93-16191
                                               CIP

Design by Robert Bull Design
Maps by Ortelius Design
Material in the Soho, Midtown, and Upper East Side tours appears courtesy of John Foreman

FROMMER'S EDITORIAL STAFF
Editorial Director: Marilyn Wood
Editorial Manager/Senior Editor: Alice Fellows
Senior Editor: Lisa Renaud
Editors: Charlotte Allstrom, Thomas F. Hirsch, Peter Katucki, Sara Hinsey
    Raveret, Theodore Stavrou
Assistant Editors: Margaret Bowen, Christopher Hollander, Ian Wilker
Editorial Assistants: Gretchen Henderson, Bethany Jewett
Managing Editor: Leanne Coupe

Special Sales
Bulk purchases of Frommer's Travel Guides are available at special discounts. The publishers are happy to custom-make publications for corporate clients who wish to use them as premiums or sales promotions. We can excerpt the contents, provide covers with corporate imprints, or create books to meet specific needs. For more information write to Special Sales, Prentice Hall Travel, Paramount Communications Building, 15 Columbus Circle, New York, NY 10023.

Manufactured in the United States of America

CONTENTS

LIST OF MAPS

A SAFETY ADVISORY

Whenever you're traveling in an unfamiliar city or country, stay alert. Be aware of your immediate surroundings. Wear a moneybelt and keep a close eye on your possessions. Be particularly careful with cameras, purses, and wallets, all favorite targets of thieves and pickpockets.

INVITATION TO THE READERS

In researching this book, I have come across many wonderful sights, shops, and restaurants, the best of which I have included here. I am sure that many of you will also discover appealing places as you explore New York. Please don't keep them to yourself. Share your experiences, especially if you want to bring to my attention information that has changed since this book was researched. You can address your letters to:

Rena Bulkin
Frommer's Walking Tours: New York
Prentice Hall Travel
15 Columbus Circle
New York, NY 10023

Introducing New York

In his novels, British humorist P. G. Wodehouse often talked about people who made the mistake of confusing the unlikely with the impossible. Obviously, these errant individuals were not New Yorkers. In the Big Apple—as in Wodehouse's anarchic world—the unlikely happens daily and the impossible with considerable regularity. To step out for a stroll on this city's streets is to stray from the rigid pathways of mundane reality. No city has New York's energy and verve—and none can match its frenetic and zany street life.

MIXED NUTS & MICHELANGELOS

For openers, a sizable cast of regular characters inhabits the city's streets. Strolling about, you might encounter the "tree man," who is always festooned with leafy branches; the portly fellow with a long white beard who dresses as Santa Claus the year round (he's Jewish, no less); or the man who pushes a baby carriage (actually it's a wheelchair with a baby carriage hood) whose occupant is a large white duck!

Probably New York's most famous character was Moondog, a hulking blind man who stood sentinel at the corner of 53rd Street and Avenue of the Americas during the 1960s—dressed as a Viking. Occasionally, journalists did stories about him, and it came out that as he stood there statuelike, leaning on a wooden staff, he was composing music in his head. On a lark, a Columbia record company executive (their offices were close by) decided to bring him into the studio to cut an album. It sold pretty well, and with the profits, Moondog bought a house upstate and retired from New York's roster of street eccentrics. There are many ways to make it in this town.

Street performers abound, too. They run the gamut from a tuxedoed gent who does Fred-and-Ginger ballroom dances with a life-size rag doll (usually in front of the Metropolitan Museum) to the circus-caliber acrobats and stand-up comics who garner large audiences in Washington Square Park. There are mimes and musicians— everything from steel-drum bands to classical string quartets to Ecuadorean flute players. If there's a line at a movie theater, chances are waiting patrons will be entertained by jugglers and fire eaters—or perhaps a pianist with his candelabra-adorned baby grand perched atop a truck.

We even have freelance street artists. You may note here and there (especially in the East Village), lovely little mosaic-tile designs adorning the sidewalk and streetlight pedestals. They're created from cracked plates and crockery by an area artist who picks up people's trash. In the early 1980s—to everyone's delight—someone printed purple footsteps and stenciled beautiful animal and fish designs on sidewalks throughout Manhattan.

One could go on ad infinitum with these New York stories. Our streets are a free outdoor theater with ongoing performances 24 hours a day. Whatever else you may feel walking around this town, you will never be bored. But even without eccentric behavior and gratis entertainment, the ever-pulsating streets of New York would yield up endless excitement.

TWIN TOWERS, TENEMENTS & TOWN HOUSES

In doing these walks, you'll come to appreciate that New York is a city of extraordinary architecture. The Financial District's neoclassic "temples"—embellished with allegorical statuary, massive colonnades, vaulted domes, and vast marble lobbies—stand side by side with the soaring skyscrapers that make up the world's most famous skyline. Close by, in the revitalized South Street Seaport district, sailing ships and seafood markets form a scenic backdrop to quaint cobblestoned streets that are lined with early 19th-century warehouses, hotels, and saloons in Georgian and Federal architectural styles. Across the nearby Brooklyn Bridge are the tranquil tree-shaded streets of Brooklyn Heights—a charming enclave of brownstones, churches, and landmark buildings, with a riverside promenade offering scenic views of the Manhattan skyline and the Statue of

Liberty. The history of immigrant groups is manifest in the ramshackle tenements of Chinatown and the Lower East Side. In Greenwich Village, you'll see the stately Greek Revival town houses where Henry James and Edith Wharton lived and wrote. SoHo is famous for 19th-century commercial buildings with ornate cast-iron facades. And uptown, magnificent private mansions built for the Vanderbilts and the Whitneys overlook Central Park, one of the world's most impressive urban greenbelts. No wonder quintessential New Yorker Woody Allen was inspired to pay loving tribute to the city's architectural diversity by including an otherwise gratuitous tour of his favorite buildings in the movie *Hannah and Her Sisters*.

THE NEIGHBORHOODS: BOK CHOY, BEADS & BOHEMIANS

Though New York has been called more of a boiling than a melting pot, its residents cherish the ethnic diversity of the city's neighborhoods. Just going from one part of town to another is an adventure almost akin to foreign travel. From the days of the early Dutch settlers, immigrants have striven to re-create their native environments in selected neighborhoods. Hence, Mulberry Street, with its convivial cafés spilling onto the sidewalk, vividly evokes the streets of Rome—especially during frequent Italian festivals when those sidewalks are crowded with vendors selling hot sausages, calzones, and cannolis.

There are two Little Indias—one along Lexington Avenue from about 27th to 30th Streets, the other, which New Yorkers call "Indian restaurant street," on East 6th Street between First and Second Avenues. The latter's cozy curry houses (there are at least a dozen) combine cheap but very hearty meals with exotic ambience— even live sitar music at dinner. The East Village also has a sizable Ukrainian population whose inexpensive restaurants, featuring borscht, blinis, and pierogis, enhance the local culinary scene. Ukrainian folk arts—such as intricately painted Easter eggs, beautifully embroidered peasant blouses, and illuminated manuscripts— are displayed in local shops and even warrant a museum on Second Avenue.

Orthodox Jews still operate shops that evolved from turn-of-the-century pushcarts along cobblestoned Orchard Street. This colorful quarter not only offers superb discount shopping—and a chance to exercise your *hondling* (bargaining) skills—it also provides an opportunity to sample the flavor of New York in the form of a pastrami on rye at Katz's Delicatessen.

Chinatown—home to over 150,000 Chinese—is probably our most extensive ethnic area, and it's continually expanding, gobbling up parts of the old Lower East Side and Little Italy. Its narrow, winding streets are lined with noodle shops, Chinese vegetable vendors, small curio stores, Buddhist temples, Chinese movie theaters, and more than four hundred restaurants. New Yorkers don't just talk about going out for Chinese food—they can opt for Szechuan, Hunan, Cantonese, Mandarin, or Fukien.

And just 20 minutes from Manhattan in Astoria, Queens, is Little Athens, where bouzouki music and the aroma of gyros and shish kebabs waft from Greek tavernas, and Greek Orthodox churches dot the area. I could go on and on. There are Latin American, Czech, German, Hungarian, Russian, Middle Eastern, and West Indian parts of town as well.

But ethnic groups are not the only factor defining New York neighborhoods. Around Broadway from Macy's to about 39th Street you're in the heart of the Garment District, where most of America's fabric and clothing designers maintain offices. In this bustling area, artists race through the streets carrying large portfolios of next season's designs, trying not to collide with workers pushing racks of already-extant clothing. Also distinct are the city's bead, book, feather, fur, flower, toy, diamond, and, of course, theater districts.

IF YOU CAN MAKE IT HERE . . .

The song has become a cliché, but like many clichés it's true. New York is, and always has been, a mecca for the ambitious. It is a city where achievement is practically a prerequisite for social acceptability. And though only a small percentage of the ardently aspiring become famous—or even manage to eke out a living in their chosen fields—the effort keeps New Yorkers keen-witted, intense, and on the cutting edge.

It's not easy to be a big fish in this pond, but for the ambitious it's the only pond really worth swimming in. New York is America's business and financial center, where major deals have gone down over power lunches since the days when Thomas Jefferson and Alexander Hamilton chose the site for the nation's capital over a meal at a Manhattan restaurant. Major book and magazine publishers are based here. It's an international media and fashion center. New York galleries set worldwide art trends. And a lead in a play in Galveston, Texas, is less impressive than a bit part on Broadway. (At least New Yorkers think so.)

For that reason, almost every famous artist, writer, musician, and actor has at one time or another resided in Gotham. The waitress serving you in a coffee shop may be tomorrow's Julia Roberts; your cab driver may make the cover of *Time* next year. And since they're all over town, you'll probably even rub elbows with an already-acclaimed celebrity or two as well. If not, there's always the thrill of downing a drink or two in bars that Dylan Thomas or Jackson Pollock frequented, visiting the Greenwich Village haunts of the Beat Generation, peering up at what was once Edgar Allan Poe's bedroom window, or dining at the Algonquin Hotel where Round Table wits Dorothy Parker, Alexander Woollcott, and George S. Kaufman traded barbs in the 1920s.

All of the above makes it very difficult for New Yorkers to find lasting happiness anywhere else. The presence of so many movers and shakers gives New York tremendous vitality and sophistication. When you study film at the New School your lecturers are Martin Scorcese, Norman Jewison, Sidney Pollack, Barry Levinson, Oliver Stone, and Neil Simon. Pavarotti's at one Met, everyone from Raphael to Rembrandt at the other. No other bookstore in America is as wonderful as the Strand, no food store as alluring as Zabar's (except perhaps Balducci's or Dean & Deluca), no department store a match for Bloomie's, no mall comparable to Orchard Street. Where else can you easily satisfy a craving for mee krob (a Thai noodle dish) at 10 o'clock in the evening? Or have your choice of dozens of movies nightly, many of which will never play in most American towns?

Visitors from the hinterlands may question how we stand the constant noise, the rudeness, the filth, the outrageous rents, the crime, the crazies, or even one another. But though New Yorkers frequently talk about leaving the city, few ever do. We've created a unique frame of reference, and it doesn't travel well. We take the bizarreness of life here and translate it into black humor. The constant stimulation feeds our creativity, and other people and places seem bland by comparison. To quote theatrical impresario Joseph Papp, "Creative people get inspiration from their immediate environment, and New York has the most immediate environment in the world."

I'm a lifelong New Yorker—one who often gripes about the city and talks of moving to more peaceful precincts. But in writing these walking tours, I've fallen in love with New York all over again. It's like a love affair with Mr. Wrong—he's moody, unpredictable, not someone you can bring home to Mom, and bad for you in the bargain—but infinitely more attractive and exciting than anyone else. Who could leave?

Getting to Know New York

To the first-time visitor, New York can be overwhelming. But there is, believe it or not, a method to the madness. The city's layout is sensible and easy to grasp. If you take just a few minutes to figure out the lay of the land, you'll soon be able to negotiate your way around like a native.

GETTING THERE

BY PLANE Almost every major international airline flies into New York (international flights usually arrive at Kennedy). Domestic carriers serving New York include **America West** (tel. toll free 800/247-5692), **American** (tel. toll free 800/433-7300), **Continental** (tel. toll free 800/525-0280), **Delta** (tel. toll free 800/221-1212), **Northwest** (tel. toll free 800/225-2525), **TWA** (tel. toll free 800/221-2000), **United** (tel. toll free 800/241-6822), and **USAir** (tel. toll free 800/428-4322).

To get the best price on your airline ticket to New York, do some comparison shopping and always ask for the lowest fare—don't just automatically accept the first price an airline quotes for you. Fares are volatile; they vary from airline to airline and even from the same

---

Ⓕ FROMMER'S SMART TRAVELER: AIRFARES

1. Use a travel agent only if you know he or she will really put in time and effort to get you the cheapest fare; otherwise, do your own homework or use a discount travel agency. It pays off!
2. Shop all the airlines that fly to New York.
3. Ask for the lowest fare, not just a discounted fare.
4. Keep calling: Airlines sometimes open up additional low-cost seats as a departure date nears.
5. Plan to travel during the week—avoid weekends and holiday periods.
6. Make sure to purchase your tickets at least 21 days in advance to take advantage of the very cheapest APEX (advance purchase) fares; next cheapest are 14-day, then 7-day advance-purchase fares.

---

airline from day to day. Try to schedule your flight on weekdays during the busy summer season and avoid major holiday periods, when fares go up. In general, the lowest fares are **Economy** or **APEX** fares—the former has no restrictions, while the latter (an Advance Purchase Excursion fare) requires you to reserve and pay for the ticket 7, 14, 21, or 30 days in advance and to stay for a minimum number of days; it also may have other restrictions, like flying before a specific date. APEX fares are usually nonrefundable, and there is a charge for changing dates; however, if you can live with these restrictions, the savings are considerable.

Keep an eye out in the travel section of your local newspaper for promotional rates. Airlines engage in cutthroat competition, and any promotional fare announced by one will probably be quickly matched by its competitors.

BY TRAIN **Amtrak** (tel. toll free 800/USA-RAIL) has frequent service to New York. If you're coming from Washington, for example, the trip will take about 3½ hours; from Boston, the travel time is about 4½ hours.

BY BUS If you've got the time, traveling by bus will be kind to your wallet. **Greyhound** (tel. 212/971-6363, or check your local listings) offers service to New York's Port Authority. From Boston, the trip might take four to five hours; from Chicago the travel time is 16 to 24 hours.

BY CAR   From the south, the New Jersey Turnpike (I-95) leads to the Holland Tunnel, the Lincoln Tunnel, and the George Washington Bridge. From the north, the New York Thruway (Rtes. 287 and 87) leads to Manhattan's East and West Sides; the New England Thruway (I-95) leads, via connecting roads, to Manhattan and the other boroughs. From the west, the Bergen-Passaic Expressway (I-80) leads to Manhattan.

I don't recommend having a car in Manhattan. Parking on the street is a hassle, and if you bring a car radio into the city, you may not have it for long. Rates for garage parking, especially in hotels, are astronomical. Don't drive here if you can avoid it.

ORIENTATION

ARRIVING

BY PLANE   New York is served by three major airports—John F. Kennedy International Airport, LaGuardia Airport, and Newark International Airport. Find your way to the Ground Transportation Center nearest your terminal; the personnel there will help you arrange transportation into the city.

Unfortunately, none of the airports is linked directly and easily to the city's public transportation network. Cabs are readily available, though, and you can try to cut costs by sharing. Be sure that you have an authorized yellow cab, and that the meter starts running accurately after you get in. It's also a good idea to get a fare receipt (you have to ask for one) so you can track down the taxi if you leave behind any of your belongings.

Buses are a much cheaper option than taxis. **Carey Airport Express** (tel. 718/632-0500) is a reliable company, with service into Manhattan every 20 to 30 minutes. You'll be dropped off at Grand Central Terminal or any one of several midtown hotels. From Newark, **Olympia Trails** (tel. 212/964-6233) will take you to the downtown World Trade Center or to Grand Central.

Minibus service is available from all airports via **Gray Line Air Shuttle** (tel. 212/757-6840), with departure schedules varying according to passenger demand.

BY TRAIN   If you're taking the train, you'll arrive at **Grand Central Terminal,** on the East Side at Park Avenue and 42nd Street, or at **Penn Station,** on the West Side at 34th Street and Seventh

Avenue. Both stations have taxi stands and easy connections with the subway system.

BY BUS   Bus travelers will arrive at New York's **Port Authority Terminal,** at Eighth Avenue and 42nd Street. The area around the terminal can be dangerous at night, so keep your wits about you. There's a taxi stand out front on Eighth Avenue, and the station is connected to several subway lines.

BY CAR   If you're driving into the city, my best advice is to find a reasonably priced place to park your car and keep it there. Street parking can be tough to find, and you may find yourself having to move your car for street cleaning every day or two.

CITY LAYOUT

NEIGHBORHOODS IN BRIEF

Lower Manhattan/Financial District   This is where you'll find Wall Street along with some of Manhattan's most historic buildings and amazing skyscrapers. Visit during the day when the financial markets are going full tilt; the area tends to be deserted at night.

TriBeCa   The "*Tri*angle *Be*low *Ca*nal Street" has followed in SoHo's footsteps in becoming a haven for artists and a trendy, revitalized neighborhood.

Lower East Side   A stroll through the Lower East Side will take you back to the turn of the century—waves of immigrants who entered the United States at Ellis Island made their first homes here. Today, an Orthodox Jewish population still thrives below Houston Street, but it shares the area with new immigrants from Latin America and Southeast Asia. Great budget shopping.

Chinatown   For street shopping and divine dining, there's no place like Chinatown, loosely bounded by Canal Street to the north, Worth Street to the South, Broadway to the West, and the Bowery to the East. It's a bustling hodgepodge of small streets lined with exotic shops and restaurants.

Little Italy   Just north of Chinatown, centered on Mulberry Street, this is the ultimate ethnic neighborhood for locals and tourists alike. The area's Italian character is reflected in its many bakeries, sidewalk cafés, restaurants, and food shops.

SoHo   "*So*uth of *Ho*uston Street" is an area extending south from Houston to Canal Street between Broadway and the Avenue of the Americas. It was an industrial and commercial neighborhood in the 19th century; its old cast-iron factory and warehouse buildings now house art galleries, and an ever-increasing number of fashionable restaurants and shops. The best sightseeing streets are West Broadway, Greene Street, Prince Street, Spring Street, and Broadway.

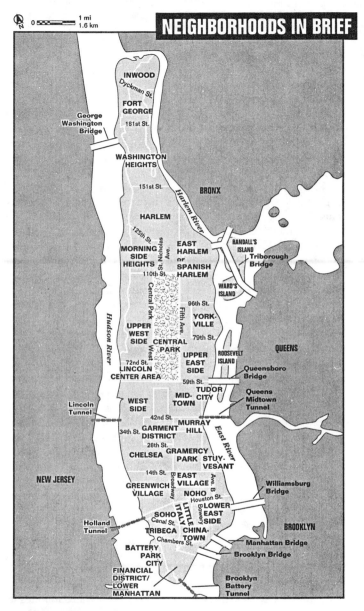

0 | 1 mi
1.6 km

INWOOD
Dyckman St.
FORT GEORGE
181st St.
George
Washington
Bridge
WASHINGTON
HEIGHTS
151st St.
Harlem River
BRONX
HARLEM
125th St.
MORNING SIDE HEIGHTS
St. Nicholas Ave.
110th St.
EAST HARLEM or SPANISH HARLEM
RANDALL'S ISLAND
Triborough Bridge
WARD'S ISLAND
Central Park West
96th St.
YORK-VILLE
Fifth Ave.
UPPER WEST SIDE
CENTRAL PARK
79th St.
Hudson River
72nd St.
UPPER EAST SIDE
ROOSEVELT ISLAND
QUEENS
LINCOLN CENTER AREA
59th St.
Queensboro Bridge
Lincoln Tunnel
WEST SIDE
MID-TOWN
TUDOR CITY
Queens Midtown Tunnel
42nd St.
34th St.
GARMENT DISTRICT
MURRAY HILL
East River
28th St.
CHELSEA
GRAMERCY PARK
STUY-VESANT
NEW JERSEY
14th St.
GREENWICH VILLAGE
Broadway
EAST VILLAGE
Ave. B
Houston St.
NOHO
Williamsburg Bridge
Holland Tunnel
SOHO
Canal St.
LITTLE ITALY
Bowery
LOWER EAST SIDE
TRIBECA
CHINA-TOWN
Chambers St.
BROOKLYN
BATTERY PARK CITY
Manhattan Bridge
Brooklyn Bridge
FINANCIAL DISTRICT/ LOWER MANHATTAN
Brooklyn Battery Tunnel

Greenwich Village   This area, still remembered for the bohemian life of the 1920s and 1930s, reflects the special diversity that is New York. The area is bounded north and south by 14th and Houston Streets, and on the east and west, respectively, by Broadway and the West Side Highway. Centered on Washington Square Park which is surrounded by New York University, it is both frenetic and serene, commercial and residential, the center of New York's gay community and home to world-famous jazz clubs. Between Seventh Avenue and Broadway you'll find Sheridan Square, honky-tonk West 4th and 8th Streets, and the whirl of Washington Square Park. Farther west there are quiet, intimate streets lined with trees and town houses.

The park is the hub of the Village—especially on a sunny weekend or a warm summer night, when it's peopled by magicians, musicians, street artists, mothers and toddlers, men bent intently over chess boards, young people on roller blades, hustlers, and hundreds of spectators soaking up the scene.

East Village In the last few years the East Village and Alphabet City, farther east, have become a magnet for artists, musicians, and punk and avant-garde style in general. It's also the center of the city's Ukrainian community. In the 1960s, St. Marks Place (an extension of 8th Street) became the center for New York's counterculture movement—the East Coast's Haight Ashbury. Since then, each new avant-garde crowd has paraded its style through the East Village's streets. Home to the New York Public Theater and other off-Broadway companies, it's also a great hunting ground for budget restaurants.

Chelsea An old residential area with the streets graced with brownstones, Chelsea has been transformed in the last two decades by trendy restaurants, theaters, and stores.

Penn Station/Herald Square/Garment District Penn Station (downstairs) and Madison Square Garden (upstairs), are located at West 34th Street between Seventh and Eighth Avenues. A couple of blocks away is Macy's in Herald Square, at the junction of Sixth Avenue, Broadway, and 34th Street. And one block farther east on Fifth Avenue stands everyone's favorite skyscraper, the Empire State Building. The wholesale shops and racks of clothes being wheeled along the street in the West 30s are a giveaway that you're in the Garment District, where a huge percentage of America's clothing is made and distributed.

Gramercy Park/Murray Hill These two East Side neighborhoods stretch from 15th Street to bustling Grand Central Terminal on 42nd Street, bounded by Park Avenue South. You'll find towering apartment complexes near the East River. There are traces of very old New York—like Irving Place, where Washington Irving used to meet with a literary salon; the Players Club, founded by Edwin Booth, still stands in all its Gothic splendor at 16 Gramercy Park South. There are contrasts—exclusive Gramercy Park and commercial areas in the 20s between Madison and Third Avenues. The Lexington Avenue section is home to many Indian and Pakistani restaurants and shops.

Midtown West/Times Square The area west of Fifth Avenue, north of 34th Street to 59th Street, is Midtown West. The

Times Square area, which occupies the blocks west of Broadway between 42nd Street to 49th Street, is, of course, home to New York's famed Broadway theater district. But it is also crammed with porno shows, pinball emporiums, pizza and souvlaki shops, and sleazy movie houses. The area is nothing if not colorful, but it can be dangerous, especially at night after the theater-going crowd has cleared off. Avoid 42nd Street between Seventh and Eighth Avenues after dark, unless you're doing a sociological study on New York's lower depths. The area is undergoing redevelopment, but all you can see of that so far is an abundance of construction sites. You'll certainly see an array of human types—preachers, streetwalkers, performers, cops, supersalesmen, pimps, office workers, out-of-towners, photographers, and just plain New Yorkers. And then of course there are the lights and billboards—block for block more here than anywhere else in the world.

Midtown-East   The area east of Fifth Avenue and north of 34th Street to 59th Street is home to countless office buildings. Walk east on 42nd Street from Grand Central Terminal and you'll pass the Chrysler Building, the Daily News Building, the Ford Foundation, en route to the United Nations at the East River's edge. A stroll up Fifth Avenue will take you close to such world-famous landmarks as Rockefeller Center, St. Patrick's Cathedral, Tiffany's, F.A.O. Schwarz, Saks Fifth Avenue, and more.

Central Park   This huge leafy oasis runs from Fifth Avenue to Central Park West and from 59th to 110th Streets—840 acres of boating, tennis, gardens, playgrounds, bridle paths, and statuary smack in the middle of some of the world's most expensive real estate. Do spend an afternoon in Central Park. You'll experience a microcosm of city life in the park, from English nannies and their charges and East Side types sunning themselves behind the Metropolitan Museum to the sounds of salsa, reggae, and rap.

Upper West Side   A former ethnic area full of mom-and-pop shops, the West Side has been gentrified as young upwardly mobile types have moved in. Some welcome the change; others deplore it. You'll find an exciting and energized neighborhood with a large student population and ethnically varied residents. Columbia University, at 116th Street between Broadway and Amsterdam Avenue, is the city's only Ivy League institution and wields considerable influence despite its distance from downtown Manhattan.

Upper East Side   East of Central ... River, between 61st and 96th Streets, this qui... the city is home to New York's "old mone... exclusive shops, art galleries, and fine antiq... Avenue. "Museum Mile" along Fifth Aven...

Metropolitan Museum of Art at 82nd Street, to El Museo del Barrio at 104th Street. In the 80s along First and Second Avenues is the area known as Yorkville, where you'll find traces of old German New York.

Harlem   For many the name is synonymous with racial tension, but for those willing to explore, there's a wealth of black culture, history, architectural restoration, and musical heritage to be found north of 110th Street.

MAIN ARTERIES & STREETS

Laid out on a grid system, Manhattan is the easiest of the boroughs to negotiate. Avenues run north (uptown) and south (downtown), while the streets run east to west (crosstown) with Fifth Avenue as the East Side/West Side demarcation. Broadway runs north to south diagonally across the grid.

Both avenues and streets are numbered consecutively, streets from south to north (1st Street is downtown just above Houston Street), and avenues from east to west, from First Avenue near the East River to Twelfth Avenue near the Hudson River. The only exceptions are the three named avenues on the East Side: Madison (next to Fifth Avenue), Park, and Lexington. Sixth Avenue is also called the Avenue of the Americas; you will see both names in these pages.

A few West Side avenues acquire new names as they move uptown: Eighth Avenue becomes Central Park West above 59th Street, Ninth Avenue becomes Columbus Avenue above 69th Street, and Tenth Avenue becomes Amsterdam above 72nd Street.

This pattern changes in the older downtown sections below 14th Street on the West Side, and below Houston Street on the East Side. Downtown streets have names rather than numbers, and in the oldest sections, streets follow the outlines of original cowpaths and old village streets. They twist and turn in no defined fashion and give such neighborhoods as Greenwich Village, Chinatown, and the Wall Street area their particular charm, but they are not as easy to negotiate.

FINDING AN ADDRESS

To find the nearest cross street on an avenue address, drop the last digit of the number of the address and divide the remaining number two. Then add or subtract the appropriate number from the list

ample, if you were trying to locate 645 Fifth Avenue, you

would drop the 5, leaving 64. Then you would divide 64 by 2, leaving 32. According to the list below, you would then add 20. Thus 645 Fifth Avenue is at about 52nd Street.

Avenue A, B, C, or D	add 3
First Avenue	add 3
Second Avenue	add 3
Third Avenue	add 10
Fourth Avenue (Park Avenue South)	add 8
Fifth Avenue	
1 to 200	add 13
201 to 400	add 16
401 to 600	add 18
601 to 775	add 20
776 to 1286	cancel last figure and subtract 18
Sixth Avenue	subtract 12
Seventh Avenue below Central Park	add 12
Eighth Avenue below Central Park	add 10
Ninth Avenue	add 13
Tenth Avenue	add 14
Eleventh Avenue	add 15
Amsterdam Avenue (Tenth Avenue above 72nd Street)	add 60
Broadway	
1 to 754 below 8th Street	
754 to 858	subtract 29
858 to 958	subtract 25
Above 1000	subtract 31
Central Park West (Eighth Avenue above 59th Street)	divide number by 10 and add 60
Columbus Avenue (Ninth Avenue above 69th Street)	add 60
Lexington Avenue	add 22
Madison Avenue	add 26
Park Avenue	add 35
Riverside Drive	divide number by 10 and add 72
West End Avenue (Eleventh Avenue above 57th Street)	add 60

All east-west street addresses in New York are counted from Fifth Avenue and increase in number as they move away from Fifth Avenue. Thus the address 2 West 44th Street would denote a building on 44th

Street just a few steps to the west of Fifth Avenue; 56 West 44th Street would indicate a building that is even farther west, and so on. The address 12 East 45th Street would denote a building just a little to the east of Fifth Avenue, while 324 East 45th Street would indicate a building on 45th Street that is much farther east of Fifth Avenue.

GETTING AROUND

BY SUBWAY Despite the noise and occasional discomfort, especially during the hottest days of summer, the quickest, cheapest, and most efficient way to move around the city is by subway. We recommend that every visitor ride the subway at least once: If you haven't ridden the subway, you haven't seen New York.

Tokens allow you to ride anywhere on the extensive system, and are obtained at token booths inside the stations. Purchase tokens with small bills; anything larger than a $20 bill will not be accepted.

To the stranger, the system might appear extremely complex and mysterious, so the first thing to do is to obtain a good map, available free at most token booths.

A number of subway lines run through Manhattan. Once the subway was separated into several systems, but today there is only one metropolitan system. The lines are the Seventh Avenue/Broadway line (1, 2, 3, and 9 trains), the Eighth Avenue line (A, C, and E trains), the Sixth Avenue line (B, D, F, and Q trains), the BMT (formerly Brooklyn-Manhattan Transit, still known by its acronym; N, R, J, M, and Z trains), and the Lexington Avenue line (4, 5, and 6 trains). Three subway lines run crosstown: the Grand Central–Times Square shuttle, the Flushing line (7 train), and the Carnarsie–14th Street line (L train). Each train is clearly numbered or lettered, indicating its specific route.

There are many crossover points from line to line; these will be indicated on your subway map. Most lines, as they pass through midtown stop at roughly similar cross streets: for example, all lines stop at 59th, 42nd, 33rd/34th, 23rd, and 14th Streets on their respective avenues and routes.

The subway is not difficult to negotiate and is a great time saver. Avoid the rush hours—8 to 9:30am and 4:30 to 6pm. Pushing and shoving is the rule then—as is most other times—but at rush hour there are at least a hundred people per car pushing and shoving (feels more like a thousand).

To avoid waiting in line to buy tokens, purchase a 10-pack. Tokens can also be used on the bus.

It is not a particularly good idea to ride very late at night. If you do, avoid empty cars and stand in the clearly designated waiting area of the station. Transit police officers patrol the trains at all times, and the conductor rides in either one of the center cars in a tiny compartment. Some station entrances are closed, and these are marked with a red light; open entrances are marked with a green light.

Do not hesitate to ask questions. Subway personnel (token sellers, conductors, transit police officers) are the best sources of information on exactly which train goes where—and how to negotiate the maze of underground passageways to find the train you're looking for, or to the exit to the street.

BY BUS The bus is the most interesting way to travel and routes are not hard to understand. Free bus maps are available. Buses require exact change in coins; the driver does not make change or take bills. Subway tokens may also be used. Transfers are free.

Virtually every avenue in Manhattan has buses that go either up or down the entire length of that avenue, in one direction since most of the avenues have one-way traffic restrictions. Buses go north (uptown) only on First Avenue, Third Avenue, Park Avenue (to 40th Street only), Madison Avenue, Sixth Avenue (Avenue of the Americas), Eighth Avenue, and Tenth Avenue.

Buses go south (downtown) only on Second Avenue, Lexington Avenue, Fifth Avenue, Broadway (below 59th Street), Seventh Avenue (below 59th Street), and Ninth Avenue.

Along York Avenue, Riverside Drive, and Broadway and Central Park West above 59th Street, buses go in both directions (uptown and downtown).

There are also a number of crosstown buses that go east or west across the entire island. Buses go east on 8th Street, 50th Street, and 65th Street. (*Important note:* This last bus travels along 65th Street on the West Side of Manhattan; after it crosses Central Park to the East Side, it continues along 65th Street to Madison Avenue, turns north for three blocks and continues east.) Buses go west only on 9th Street, 49th Street, and 67th Street. (*Another important note:* This last bus travels along 67th Street on the East Side of Manhattan only; after it crosses Central Park to the West Side, it continues its westbound route on 66th Street.)

Buses go in both directions (east and west) on 14th Street, 23rd Street, 34th Street, 42nd Street, 57th Street, 59th Street, 79th Street, 86th Street, 96th Street, 116th Street, 125th Street, 145th Street, and 155th Street.

Free transfers can only be used where routes intersect (ask for

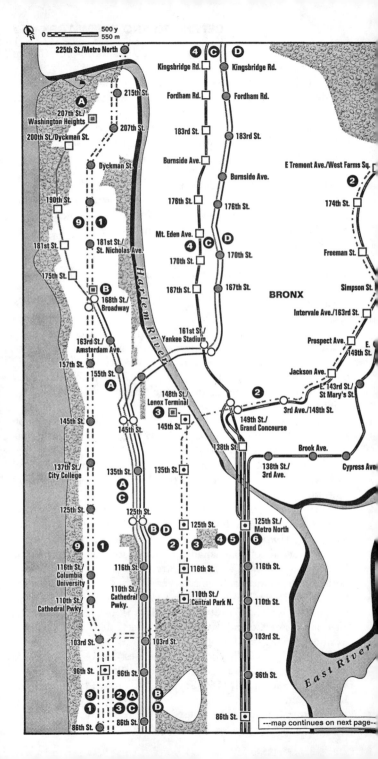

225th St./Metro North

Kingsbridge Rd. ▣ ● Kingsbridge Rd.

4 C D

215th St.

Fordham Rd. ▣ ● Fordham Rd.

207th St./
Washington Heights

A

200th St./Dyckman St.
207th St.

183rd St. ▣ ● 183rd St.

Dyckman St.

Burnside Ave. ▣

190th St.

E Tremont Ave./West Farms Sq.

2

Burnside Ave. ●

9 1

176th St. ▣ ● 176th St.

174th St.

181st St.

181st St./
St. Nicholas Ave.

Mt. Eden Ave. ▣

4 C D

175th St.

170th St. ▣ ● 170th St.

Freeman St.

B

167th St. ▣ ● 167th St.

Simpson St.

168th St./
Broadway

BRONX

163rd St./
Amsterdam Ave.

161st St./
Yankee Stadium

Intervale Ave./163rd St.

157th St.

Prospect Ave.

155th St.

E.
149th St.

A

Jackson Ave.

148th St./
Lenox Terminal

2

E. 143rd St./
St Mary's St.

145th St.

3

3rd Ave./149th St.

145th St.

145th St.

149th St./
Grand Concourse

138th St.

Brook Ave. ● ●

137th St./
City College

135th St.

135th St.

138th St./
3rd Ave.

Cypress Ave

A
C

125th St.

125th St.

B D

125th St.

2

125th St./
Metro North

9 1

2 3

4 5

6

116th St./
Columbia
University

116th St.

116th St.

116th St.

110th St./
Cathedral Pwky.

110th St./
Cathedral
Pwky.

110th St./
Central Park N.

110th St.

103rd St.

103rd St.

103rd St.

East River

96th St.

96th St.

96th St.

9

2 A

B

1

3 C

D

86th St.

86th St.

86th St.

---map continues on next page---

500 y
0 ■■■■■
550 m

Harlem River

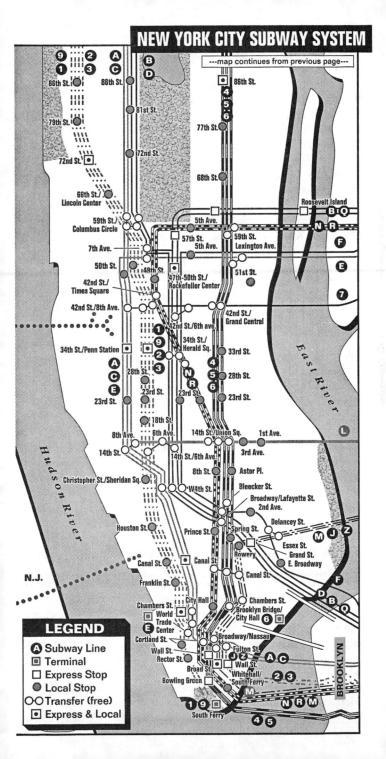

NEW YORK CITY SUBWAY SYSTEM

---map continues from previous page---

your transfer when you pay your fare as bus drivers often get cranky if asked later).

BY TAXI Obviously the most convenient way to travel around town is by cab, but it's not cheap. As of this writing, there is a 50¢ surcharge tacked on each fare from 8pm to 6am. Of course you are also expected to tip, but don't let any driver intimidate you—give around 15% on all fares.

On short rides, if a group of people hop a cab together it can often cost less than taking a subway.

Although it's usually easy enough to walk out and hail a passing cab, there may be occasions when you'd prefer door-to-door service. Check the *Yellow Pages* under the heading "Taxicab Service" for radio-dispatched cabs, which operate on regular meter rates, though sometimes there's an extra charge if you reserve in advance.

Cabs are hard to come by during morning and evening rush hours, and furthermore any trip at these times will cost you a fortune in waiting time. It's also hard to find a cab in inclement weather.

Avoid gypsy cabs. These cabs do not have a medallion on top, many have a battered appearance, and they offer somewhat question-able service. There are, however, some fine private-car services with radio-dispatched late-model sedans. If you find yourself in an area not serviced by regular yellow cabs, ask a local person for a recommenda-tion or check the *Yellow Pages* under "Car Service" or "Taxis." Ask for the rate when booking service.

BY CAR Try to avoid driving in Manhattan. Drivers are aggressive, street parking is close to impossible, and garage parking is expensive. Illegally parked cars are towed, and you will have to pay a stiff fine to recover your vehicle. People in New York have been known to have fistfights over street-side parking places. If you're very lucky, you may catch someone leaving a spot; otherwise, you'll need to keep circling. Don't wait to see a car pulling out. Watch for telltale signs—a person reaching into a pocket for keys, opening a car door, or walking purposefully toward a vehicle.

The main office of the **American Automobile Association (AAA)** in Manhattan is at Broadway and 62nd Street (tel. 757-2000).

The major **national car rental** companies, such as Avis, Budget, National, and Hertz, all have branches in Manhattan, but be prepared for sky-high rates.

SUBURBAN TRANSIT New York has excellent rail connec-tions to its suburbs and other major cities in the Northeast. For Metro North information (for Westchester County and other north-ern suburbs), dial 532-4900; phone 718/217-5477 for Long Island

Rail Road information (for all of Long Island); call toll free 800/USA-RAIL for Amtrak information.

FAST FACTS NEW YORK

American Express American Express Travel Services has several offices around Manhattan, including the following: 150 East 42nd Street (tel. 687-3700); in Bloomingdales, at Lexington Avenue and 59th Street (tel. 705-3171); in Macy's, at Herald Square (tel. 695-8075); and in the World Financial Center (tel. 640-5130).

Area Code The area code for Manhattan and the Bronx is 212; for Queens, Staten Island, and Brooklyn it's 718; for Long Island it's 516; for Westchester and Rockland counties it's 914; for suburban Connecticut it's 203; and for New Jersey it's 201, 908, or 609.

Bookstores It would be impossible to list all of New York's bookstores here, so what follows is only a very abbreviated list of some of the more interesting offerings: Applause Theatre Books, 211 West 71st Street, between Broadway and West End Avenue (tel. 496-7511); the Barnes & Noble Annex, Fifth Avenue between 17th and 18th Streets (tel. 633-3500); Brentano's Bookstore, 597 Fifth Avenue, between 48th and 49th Streets (tel. 826-2450); Eeyore's Books for Children, 25 East 83rd Street, between Fifth and Madison Avenues (tel. 988-3404); the Gotham Bookmart, 41 West 47th Street, between Fifth and Sixth Avenues (tel. 719-4448); Murder, Inc., 2486 Broadway, between 92nd and 93rd Streets (tel. 362-8905); Rizzoli Bookstore, 31 West 57th Street, between Fifth and Sixth Avenues (tel. 759-2424); Shakespeare & Co., 2259 Broadway, at 81st Street (tel. 580-7800); the Strand, 828 Broadway, at 12th Street (tel. 473-1452); and the Oscar Wilde Memorial Bookshop, 15 Christopher Street (tel. 255-8097).

Business Hours Standard office hours are 9am to 5pm. Banks in Manhattan keep relatively short hours, closing on most weekdays at 3 or 3:30pm. Department stores are usually open until 6pm, with late closings (usually around 8:30pm on Mondays and Thursdays). Bars and restaurants keep late hours, with a good number of eateries open around the clock to satisfy late-night cravings.

Climate New York's weather is nothing if not fickle. In winter the wind can be bitterly cold or you could be in for mild sunny skies. (Summers tend to be universally humid and muggy.) Your best bet is to dress in layers and to keep an eye on each day's weather forecast.

Currency Exchange There are branches of Thomas Cook Currency Services at several locations around Manhattan, including the JFK Airport International Arrivals Building, Rockefeller Center, and Grand Central Terminal.

Dentists The Emergency Dental Service (tel. 679-3966, or 679-4172 after 8pm) is a 24-hour answering service that will try to refer you to a dentist.

Doctors Manhattan Medical Care, 116 West 72nd Street (tel. 496-9620) will accept walk-ins. House calls are available from Doctors on Call (tel. 718/238-2100).

Drugstores Duane Reade stores, located throughout the city, offer discount prices. A good drugstore (with a pharmacy) that's open 24 hours a day is Kaufman's, 50th Street and Lexington Avenue (tel. 755-2266). Many Love Stores are also open around the clock.

Embassies/Consulates The Australian consulate is located at 636 Fifth Avenue (tel. 245-4000); the Canadian consulate is at 1251 Avenue of the Americas (tel. 768-2400); the Irish consulate is located at 515 Madison Avenue (tel. 319-2555); and the British consulate is at 845 Third Avenue (tel. 745-0202).

Emergencies Call the police, the fire department, or an ambulance at 911.

Eyeglasses Lenscrafters has two centrally located branches, at 901 Sixth Avenue at 33rd Street and 2040 Broadway at 70th Street, both offering one-hour service.

Hospitals Emergency wards are always open at St. Vincent's Hospital, Seventh Avenue and 11th Street (tel. 790-7000); New York Hospital, East 70th Street at York Avenue (tel. 746-5454); Mt. Sinai Hospital, Madison Avenue and 100th Street (tel. 241-7171); St. Luke's Roosevelt Hospital, 58th Street and Ninth Avenue (tel. 523-4000); and New York University Medical Center, First Avenue and 33rd Street (tel. 263-7300).

Hotlines The Gay/Lesbian Switchboard (tel. 777-1800) operates daily and has listings for organizations and agencies that deal with gay issues. Alcoholics Anonymous can be reached at 473-6200. The Helpline (tel. 532-2400), Victims Services (tel. 577-7777), or The Samaritans (tel. 673-3000) are available for help and counseling 24 hours a day.

Libraries The main branch of the New York Public Library is at Fifth Avenue and 42nd Street.

Maps Subway maps are free and available at most stations.

Newspapers/Magazines New York has four major daily newspapers, the *New York Times,* the *Daily News,* the *New York Post,* and *New York Newsday.* The Friday "Weekend" and the Sunday "Arts and Leisure" sections of the *Times* are especially good resources. Weekly publications with good entertainment and cultural listings include the *New Yorker, New York* magazine, and the *Village Voice* (which is particularly strong for music, cheap events, freebies, and off- and off-off-Broadway performances). You'll find newsstands on practically every corner.

Photographic Needs Dozens of cut-rate photo-supply stores dot the West Side. One of the best known is 47th Street Photo, at 67 West 47th Street, between Fifth and Sixth Avenues (tel. 260-4410).

Police Call 911 for serious emergencies only; call 374-5000 for other matters.

Post Office The main branch of the post office is at 33rd Street and Eighth Avenue (tel. 967-8585); it's open 24 hours.

Restrooms Many restaurants reserve their restrooms for customers' use only; you can generally just buy a soda or a cup of coffee to get around this restriction. All the major department stores are good bets, and you can also use the facilities in the lobbies of most of the better hotels.

Safety New York's reputation as a dangerous city is not entirely undeserved, but by using common sense you can minimize your chances of becoming a crime victim. It is your responsibility to stay alert in what may seem the safest situation. When strolling New York streets alone at night, stay in areas where there are lots of people. Traveling in a group is always safer.

Some areas should be avoided entirely at night, including Harlem, Times Square (except during theater hours), the section of the East Village known as "Alphabet City," and the Lower East Side.

Walk purposefully. Wear a moneybelt or at least make sure that your purse isn't dangling loosely. Don't wear expensive jewelry or keep passports and all your money in a single place.

In the subway, don't stand close to the tracks. Choose crowded, not empty, cars, and once riding, stay alert and beware of pickpockets. The subways aren't recommended for late-night travel.

Taxes New York sales tax is 8¼%.

Tourist Information Stop by the New York Convention and Visitors Bureau at 2 Columbus Circle (West 59th Street and Broadway), open from 9am to 6pm Monday through Friday. The staff is knowledgeable, and there's a wealth of brochures and information on attractions and special events.

Transit Information For bus or subway information, call 718/330-1234.

~~~

Lower Manhattan/The Financial District

~~~

Start: The Municipal Building, at Centre and Chambers Streets.
Subway: Take the 4, 5, or 6 to Brooklyn Bridge/City Hall, or take the R to City Hall. (You can also catch an M–15 City Hall bus on Second Avenue.)
Finish: The New York Stock Exchange.
Time: Approximately 3 to 4 hours.
Best Times: Any weekday, when the wheels of finance are spinning and lower Manhattan is a maelstrom of frantic activity.
Worst Times: Weekends, when most buildings are closed.

The winding narrow streets of the Financial District occupy the earliest-settled area of Manhattan, where the Dutch established the colony of New Amsterdam in 1612. Here colonial, 18th-century Georgian-Federal, and 19th-century neoclassical buildings stand in the shadow of the colossal skyscrapers that form the silhouette of the world's most famous skyline. To best view the buildings described below, stand far back to gain aesthetic perspective, then closely inspect the architectural details of the facades and interior spaces.

REFRESHMENT STOP   Consider starting out early with breakfast at **Ellen's Café & Bake Shop,** 270 Broadway at Chambers Street (tel. 962-1257). Owner Ellen Hart was Miss Subways in 1959 (it was a New York beauty contest), and her restaurant walls are lined with other Miss Subways posters and photographs of all the politicians who eat here—Al D'Amato, David Dinkins, Bella Abzug, Mario Cuomo, and Geraldine Ferraro, to name a few. Muffins, biscuits, and pastries are all oven-fresh.

---

1. **The Municipal Building,** a grand civic edifice built between 1909 and 1914 to augment City Hall's government office space, was designed by the famed architectural firm of McKim, Mead, and White (as in Stanford White). They utilized Greek and Roman design elements such as a massive Corinthian colonnade, ornately embellished vaults and cornices, and allegorical statuary. A triumphal arch, its barrel-vaulted ceiling adorned with bas-relief panels, forms a magnificent arcade over Chambers Street that has been called the "gate of the city." Sculptor Adolph Weinman created many of the bas reliefs as well as the heroic copper statue of *Civic Fame* crowning the structure.

   See many lovey-dovey couples walking in and out? The city's marriage license bureau is on the second floor, and a wedding takes place about every 20 minutes in the chapel across the hall.

   Walk west on Chambers Street to:

2. **Surrogate's Court (The Hall of Records),** 31 Chambers Street. Housed in this sumptuous turn-of-the-century beaux arts structure are all the legal records relating to Manhattan real estate deeds and court cases, some dating back to the mid-1600s. Heroic statues of distinguished New Yorkers front the mansard roof, and the doorways, surmounted by arched pediments, are flanked by Philip Martiny's sculptural groups portraying *New York in Revolutionary Times* and *New York in Its Infancy.* Above the entrance is a three-story colonnade.

   Do walk inside to see the lobby's arched mosaic Egyptian-motif ceiling and beautiful murals. Continue back to the three-story skylit central hall and ornate staircase adapted from the foyer of the Grand Opera House in Paris.

   Across the street at 52 Chambers is:

3. **Tweed Courthouse (New York County Courthouse).** This 1872 Italianate courthouse was built during the tenure of William Marcy "Boss" Tweed, who, in his post on the Board of Supervisors, stole millions from its construction funds. Though it was originally budgeted as a $250,000 job in 1861, the price tag escalated to the staggering sum (for the 19th century) of $14 million. Bills were padded to an unprecedented extent. For instance, Andrew Garvey, who was to become known as the "Prince of Plasterers" was ostensibly paid $45,966.89 for a single

day's work! The ensuing scandal (Tweed and his cronies, it came out, had pocketed at least $10 million) wrecked Tweed's career, and he died penniless in jail.

Walking west toward Broadway, make a left into:

4. **City Hall Park,** a 250-year-old green surrounded by landmark buildings. It is the setting for:

5. **City Hall,** the seat of municipal government, housing the offices of the mayor and his staff, the City Council, and other vital city agencies. Its elegant architecture combines Georgian and French-Renaissance styles. It was on this site (then the City Common) that George Washington read the Declaration of Independence on July 9, 1776, officially bringing New York into the Revolutionary War. Lincoln lay in state outside City Hall after his assassination. And it is on City Hall steps that New York mayors bestow the keys to the city on honored guests.

The eastern boundary of City Hall Park is:

6. **Park Row.** In the early 20th century, 12 New York City newspapers—all the great metropolitan dailies—maintained offices on this street. On the other side of the park is the:

7. **Woolworth Building,** 233 Broadway. This soaring "Cathedral of Commerce" cost Frank W. Woolworth $13 million worth of nickels and dimes in 1913 (he paid cash). Designed by Cass Gilbert, it was, until 1930, the world's tallest building. The architectural style is Neo-Gothic, with spires, gargoyles, flying buttresses, lace-in-stone traceries, castlelike turrets, and a churchlike interior. At its opening, President Woodrow Wilson pressed a button from the White House that illuminated the Woolworth Building's 80,000 electric light bulbs! Step into the lofty marble entrance arcade to view the vaulted gleaming mosaic ceiling and gold-leafed cornices. The carved figures under the cross beams include portraits of Woolworth (counting change) and Gilbert (holding a miniature model of the building).

Continue walking downtown on Broadway to:

8. **St. Paul's Chapel,** on Broadway between Vesey and Fulton Streets. During the two years that New York was the nation's capital, George Washington worshipped at this 1766 Georgian chapel of Trinity Church. His pew is on one side of the church, the governor's on the opposite side. Pierre Charles L'Enfant (who laid out the city of Washington, D.C.) designed the gilded sunburst above the altar. Before landfill gave the island of Manhattan its current shape, the Hudson used to flow next to St. Paul's. Do explore the small graveyard where 18th- and early 19th-century notables are buried. There are chamber music and orchestral concerts here at noon most Mondays and Thursdays.

Just downtown from St. Paul's stands the:

9. **A T & T Building,** at 195 Broadway. This early 20th-century (1915–22) neoclassical telecommunications tower has more exterior columns than any other building in the world. The 25-story structure rests on a Doric colonnade, with Ionic colonnades above, and the massively columned lobby evokes a Greek temple. The building's tower crown is modeled on the Mausoleum of Halicarnassus, one of the great Greek monuments of antiquity. Bronze panels over the entranceway by Paul Manship (sculptor of Rockefeller Center's Prometheus) symbolize wind, air, fire, and earth. No longer A T & T headquarters, the building is today the Kalikow Building.

Make a right on Dey Street. Up ahead—you can't miss it—is the:

10. **World Trade Center,** bounded by Vesey, West, Liberty, and Church Streets and best known for its famous 110-story twin towers. Still intact despite a terrorist bombing in early 1993, the WTC comprises an immense office complex (boasting 10 million square feet and housing over 1,200 businesses) under the auspices of the Port Authority. Opened in the early seventies, it occupies 16 acres and includes, in addition to the towers, the sleek Vista Hotel, a plaza the size of four football fields (used for concerts, picnicking, and special events), an underground shopping mall, and several restaurants, most notably the rooftop Windows on the World. Though the twin towers of the World Trade Center have become a distinctive feature of the Manhattan skyline, not everyone is impressed by them. Architecture critic Paul Goldberger, in *The City Observed,* called them "so banal as to be unworthy of the headquarters of a bank in Omaha."

The thing to do, of course, is whiz up to the 107th-floor observation deck. From there be sure to ascend to the 110th-floor promenade for magnificent al fresco views. Observation facilities are open daily from 9:30am to 9:30pm (tickets can be purchased on the mezzanine level of Two World Trade Center).

REFRESHMENT STOPS For a quick meal, there's a snack bar on the 107th-floor observation deck of the World Trade Center.

To enjoy those 107th-floor views, consider **Windows on the World,** One World Trade Center (tel. 938-1111). The fare is American/continental, the average check per person about $30. Reservations are suggested. Open for lunch daily from noon to 2:15pm.

In the same price bracket, another lovely choice is the elegant and charming **American Harvest Restaurant** (tel. 432-

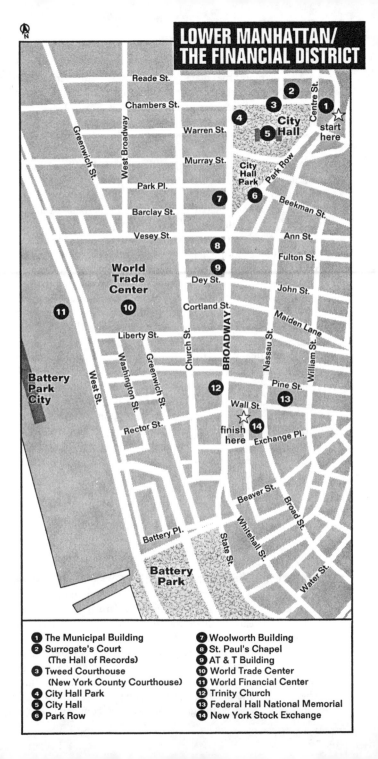

LOWER MANHATTAN/ THE FINANCIAL DISTRICT

Reade St.
Chambers St.
Warren St.
Murray St.
Park Pl.
Barclay St.
Vesey St.
Dey St.
Cortland St.
Liberty St.
Rector St.
Battery Pl.

Greenwich St.
West Broadway
Church St.
BROADWAY
Nassau St.
Centre St.
Park Row
Beekman St.
Ann St.
Fulton St.
John St.
Maiden Lane
William St.
Pine St.
Wall St.
Exchange Pl.
Washington St.
Greenwich St.
West St.
Beaver St.
Whitehall St.
Broad St.
State St.
Water St.

City Hall
City Hall Park
World Trade Center
Battery Park City
Battery Park

start here
finish here

① The Municipal Building
② Surrogate's Court (The Hall of Records)
③ Tweed Courthouse (New York County Courthouse)
④ City Hall Park
⑤ City Hall
⑥ Park Row
⑦ Woolworth Building
⑧ St. Paul's Chapel
⑨ AT & T Building
⑩ World Trade Center
⑪ World Financial Center
⑫ Trinity Church
⑬ Federal Hall National Memorial
⑭ New York Stock Exchange

9334) on the plaza level of the Vista Hotel in the WTC complex. Fare is American regional.

Also explore the many dining options—in varied price ranges, some with outdoor seating overlooking the yacht basin—at the World Financial Center (see Stop 11). You can pick up a brochure at the entrance that lists them all.

Across the West Side Highway but reachable via an indoor walkway from the WTC is the:

11. World Financial Center, a dramatic office complex centered on the enormous glass-enclosed Winter Garden—a barrel-vaulted "crystal palace" filled with towering palms, each over 60 feet tall. Adjoining arcades house about 50 shops and restaurants, and a beautifully landscaped esplanade overlooks a yacht basin. An ongoing schedule of events, concerts, and exhibits takes place here—everything from jazz concerts to photography shows. Call 945-0505 to find out what's on during your visit.

Walk back to Church Street, make a left on Liberty Street to Broadway, and continue downtown a couple of blocks to:

12. Trinity Church, Broadway and Wall Street. Serving God and Mammon, this Wall Street house of worship—with Gothic flying buttresses, beautiful stained-glass windows, and vaulted ceilings—was built in 1846. Its main doors are modeled after the famed Ghiberti doors found on the Baptistry in Florence.

The original church on this site went up in 1697 and burned down in 1776 during the Revolution. This first structure stood just outside a massive wall marking the boundaries of the Dutch settlement—hence the name Wall Street. In the churchyard, where the oldest grave dates to 1681, are the burial sites of steamboat inventor Robert Fulton, Alexander Hamilton, and Captain James Lawrence (whose famous last words were "Don't give up the ship."). You can pick up a graveyard map on the premises. A brief lecture tour is given weekdays at 2pm, and there's a small historical museum on the premises.

Make a left into Wall Street and walk one block to the:

13. Federal Hall National Memorial, 26 Wall Street at Nassau Street. Fronted by 32-foot fluted marble Doric columns, this imposing 1842 Greek Revival building is largely famous for the history of an earlier edifice that occupied the site. It was there that Peter Zenger, publisher of the *Weekly Journal,* stood trial in 1735 for libeling the Royal Governor; his acquittal set the precedent for freedom of the press, which was later guaranteed in the Bill of Rights. Congress met there after the Revolution, when New York was briefly the nation's capital. And an 1883 statue of George Washington on the steps commemorates his inauguration at this site in 1789. Exhibits within elucidate these events along with other aspects of American history. Admission is free.

Cross Wall Street, where Nassau changes to Broad Street, and head to the Visitors' Center entrance of the:

14. New York Stock Exchange, 20 Broad Street. The New York Stock Exchange came into being in 1792 for the purpose of selling government bonds to pay Revolutionary War debts. Today, America's financial nerve center is housed in this 1903 beaux arts "temple" with a pediment sculpture depicting (Michael Milken take note) *Integrity Protecting the Works of Man.* Over two thousand companies are listed on the exchange; they have a combined value of about $4 trillion!

On self-guided tours departing weekdays between 9:15am and 4pm, you can learn all about stock trading, view exhibits— and a short film— on the history and workings of the stock market, and watch the frenzied action on the trading floor. The observation platform has been glassed in since the 1960s, when Abbie Hoffman and Jerry Rubin created chaos by tossing dollar bills onto the exchange floor. Ticket distribution begins at 9am. There's no charge for the tour at this writing, but admission is being considered.

To reach Fraunces Tavern continue south on Broad Street.

REFRESHMENT STOP Fraunces Tavern, 54 Pearl Street (tel. 269-0144), is listed here as a place to eat, but it could also be a stop on the tour. Situated on a historic block that's lined with 18th- and 19th-century buildings, it is a 1907 reconstruction of the 1719 Étienne De Lancey mansion that first occupied this site. In 1762 Samuel Fraunces bought the property and converted it to the Queen's Head Tavern, where George Washington bade farewell to his officers in 1783 following America's victory in the Revolutionary War. During the 19th century, the building suffered the ravages of several fires. In 1904, the Sons of the Revolution purchased and restored it based on typical period buildings rather than exact specifications.

The main floor today contains a very charming—but expensive—oak-paneled dining room with a working fireplace. It features steak, seafood, and colonial fare such as Yankee pot roast. Or you can opt for more moderately priced pub fare in the Tap Room, which has plush leather furnishings and walls hung with historic American flags and African hunting trophies. Reservations are suggested at both spots; better yet, arrive off-hours to avoid crowds. The restaurant is open weekdays for breakfast from 7:30 to 10:30am and for lunch from 11:30am to 4pm; the Tap Room is open from 11:30am to 9:30pm.

The two upper stories house the Fraunces Tavern Museum, where you can view the room where Washington's farewell took place, and see other exhibits on American history. Admission is charged. Hours are Monday through Friday from 10am to 4:45pm, and Saturdays from noon to 4pm.

~~~~~~~~

South Street Seaport

~~~~~~~~

Start: Fulton Fish Market.
Subway: Take the 2, 3, 4, 5, J, or M to Fulton Street.
Finish: The *Titanic* Memorial Lighthouse.
Time: 3 hours, not including time for shopping and refreshments.
Best Times: Very early in the morning, when the fish market is buzzing with activity; or weekday afternoons.

Once the heart of New York's booming shipping industry, the South Street Seaport is a 12-square-block Landmark Historic District that's been brought back to life by a massive revitalization effort. In the 1800s, these quaint cobblestone streets near the East River were crowded with sailors and merchants who made their living importing exotic treasures from China, India, and Java. Today, you're more likely to spot Wall Street bankers and well-heeled tourists in the restaurants and galleries that now occupy the Seaport's restored 19th-century row houses, warehouses, saloons, and hotels—but with a little imagination, you can feel yourself transported back to the days of the tall ships that made New York a great center for trade.

From the subway station, walk east on Fulton Street (away from the World Trade Center towers), crossing Pearl Street. From 1686 until around 1820, landfill was used to build up the island of Manhattan. Though it's now three blocks inland, Pearl Street, believe it or not, was once part of Manhattan's original eastern shoreline.

Fulton Street (once called Beekman Slip but renamed in 1816 to honor Robert Fulton) was filled in around 1811. Its terminus was chosen as the Manhattan landing of Robert Fulton's Brooklyn ferry; the ferry traffic was largely responsible for making Fulton Street a major thoroughfare.

Continue on Fulton Street, heading toward the water and under the highway overpass to our first stop, the:

1. **Fulton Fish Market,** the largest wholesale fish market in the country. If you're visiting in the early morning, don't lose any time in making your way here (if you arrive after 11am, the market will have died down and you can skip ahead to Stop 2). In the predawn hours, while most of the city is still asleep, the market comes to life, as the catch of the day—tuna, mackerel, halibut, crab, sole, and much, much more—is brought in, iced, unpacked, and displayed for retailers and restauranteurs. When the bustling and bargaining are underway, it's sheer bedlam.

   When you leave the market, retrace your steps on Fulton Street to the:

2. **South Street Seaport Museum Visitors' Center,** where you can browse through a photographic exhibit documenting the Seaport's maritime heritage and the restoration effort that began to bring the area back to life in the 1960s. Here you can also purchase tickets to tour the museum's historic ships, join an organized walking tour of the area, or arrange to take a Seaport Line harbor cruise or a sail on the schooner *Pioneer.* An orientation stop here is highly recommended, since the museum offers a frequently changing program of walking tours, concerts, seminars, and workshops covering everything from printing with antique hand-set type to ship restoration.

   Exit the Visitors' Center, and once you're out on Fulton Street, step back and admire the 19th-century facades along:

3. **Schermerhorn Row,** the architectural centerpiece of the Seaport. This block, originally built in late Georgian-Federal style as a series of storehouses with merchants' counting rooms, was constructed in 1811 to 1812 for Peter Schermerhorn, a wealthy ship's chandler.

   Across the way is:

4. **21–25 Fulton Street.** Built in 1846, these Greek Revival–style stores were constructed for merchant George Rogers; today, they're occupied by Ann Taylor and Caswell-Massey.

   Make a 180° turn and head toward Front Street. The 19th- and 20th-century buildings that line this block are now occupied by upscale shops such as Coach Leatherware and Country Road Australia. To your right is One Seaport Plaza, a modern structure that provides a stark contrast to its small 19th-century neighbors. Here you'll see:

5. **Abercrombie & Fitch,** one of the legendary names in New York's retail world. Stop in and browse for outdoorsy, L. L. Bean–style sportswear.

Continue on Front Street and make a left when you reach John Street. On the left side of the street is the:

6. **Children's Center,** where your kids will delight in the hands-on workshops and holiday and maritime programs. Perhaps they'll decorate a Halloween pumpkin, craft a sailboard kite, travel around the world using giant puzzle pieces, or learn how fish travel from the sea to their supper plates. (Advance reservations are suggested for most programs; call 669-9400 before you visit to see what's happening.)

Just past the Children's Center, at 167–171 John Street, is the:

7. **A. A. Low Building,** where A. A. Low & Co., a prominent firm in the China trade, was housed from 1850 to the early 20th century. The Lows commissioned the building of the *Hoqua* in 1844, and with its completion, the era of the "China Clipper" was begun. The company imported exotic cargo from the Orient—fabrics, porcelains, spices, and tea—and was among the first to send ships to Japan. The gallery that's housed here today displays various maritime exhibits.

At the corner of John Street and South Street is the:

8. **Boat Building Shop,** where skilled craftspeople build and restore wooden vessels. Occasional boat-building courses are offered (call 742-1116 in advance of your visit for details).

REFRESHMENT STOPS **Sloppy Louie's,** 92 South Street (tel. 952-9657), has been an institution at the Seaport since 1930, serving fresh, hearty seafood in an unpretentious setting. You might start with plump, juicy scallops or a crabmeat cocktail before moving on to a main course like the fresh Atlantic bluefish. The house specialty is bouillabaisse, available as an appetizer or in a portion large enough to serve as your main course. Prices are moderate.

Next door, at 93 South Street, is the **North Star Pub** (tel. 509-6757), a must for Anglophiles who have a craving for shepherd's pie or bangers and mash. The North Star proudly proclaims that it serves no domestic beers—North Star hard cider, Guinness, and scotch are the drinks of choice. Don't forget to finish off your meal with the very-deep-dish apple pie

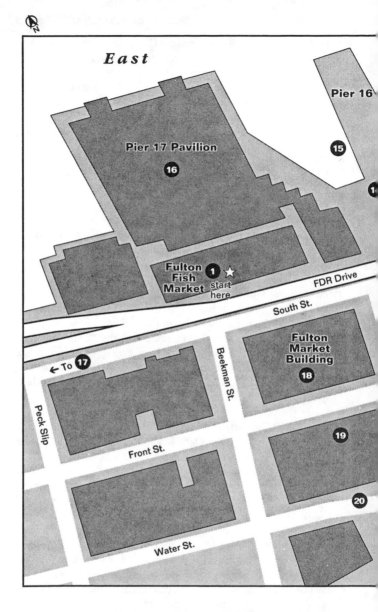

East

Pier 16

Pier 17 Pavilion
16

15

Fulton Fish Market 1 ★ start here

FDR Drive

South St.

← To 17

Fulton Market Building 18

Beekman St.

Peck Slip

Front St.

19

20

Water St.

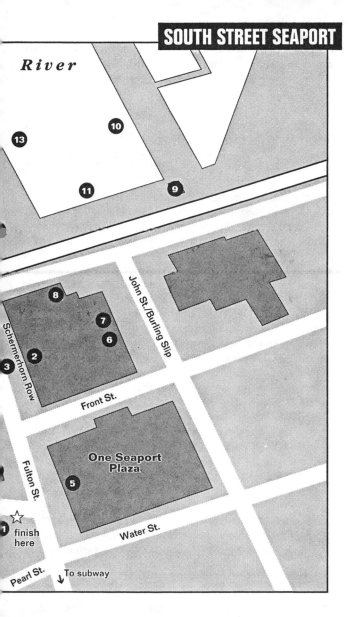

SOUTH STREET SEAPORT

River

13 **10**

11 **9**

John St./Burling Slip

8

7

6

Schermerhorn Row

2

3

Front St.

One Seaport Plaza

5

Fulton St.

☆ **1** finish here

Water St.

Pearl St.

↓ To subway

---

12 Pier 16 Ticketbooth
13 *Peking*
14 The Pilothouse
15 *Ambrose*
16 Pier 17 Pavilion

17 Meyer's Hotel
18 Fulton Market Building
19 J. Crew
20 Water Street
21 *Titanic* Memorial Lighthouse

(topped with cheddar cheese or Devon cream, of course). You can expect to pay less than $20 for lunch and a drink.

Cross South Street, heading under the overpass, and make your way to the:

9. Maritime Crafts Center, where you'll see carvers, painters, and artisans at work on models, ship carvings, and figureheads.

Head out onto the pier just past the Crafts Center. The tall ship before you is the:

10. *Wavertree,* an impressive three-masted, iron-hulled ship that dates back to 1885. It was once used in the jute trade between India and Europe, and in its day, it sailed the high seas to ports in Australia and South America. The *Wavertree*'s main mast snapped off during a storm while the ship was rounding Cape Horn in 1910, and from 1911 to 1948, the damaged vessel was used as an anchored storage hulk in the Strait of Magellan. In 1968, the Seaport Museum purchased the *Wavertree,* and its ongoing renovation is one of the major achievements of the Seaport's ship restoration program.

Retrace your steps back to the Crafts Center, and then head toward Pier 16, where vessels of every description—whaling ships, clippers, and steamers—once docked during the Seaport's golden age. On the way, you'll pass the:

11. *Lettie G. Howard,* a restored Gloucester fishing schooner that was built in Essex, Massachusetts, in 1893. Many such vessels used to haul their catches into the Fulton Market each day.

If the sight of the Seaport's ships has given you a yearning to head out onto the high seas, head now for the:

12. Pier 16 Ticketbooth. If you didn't stop in at the Visitors' Center at the beginning of our tour, here's another chance to purchase tickets to tour the Seaport Museum's ships, arrange to take a harbor cruise, or sign up for a sail on the schooner *Pioneer.* Free outdoor concerts are often held on summer evenings in the area just past the ticketbooth—performers such as Bo Diddley, the Boys Choir of Harlem, Judy Collins, and the U.S. Coast Guard Band have played here.

Just ahead and to your right is anchored the:

13. *Peking,* a magnificent four-masted, 347-foot bark built in Germany in 1911, with a mast that towers more than 170 feet above the deck. Once sporting more than an acre of sail when it journeyed across the high seas, the *Peking* was fast and trim, designed to make the difficult and dangerous journey around Cape Horn.

The ship carried general cargo from Europe to the west coast of South America and returned with loads of nitrates (used for fertilizer). With the advent of synthetic fertilizers, the ship's owner found his usual run no longer profitable; in 1931 he sold the *Peking* to a British boys' school, where it was used as a training ship. It remained in Britain until the Seaport Museum bought it in 1974. The *Peking* has been restored and rerigged so that it looks much today as it did in its prime.

Just beside the *Peking* is the old:

14. **Pilothouse,** which once belonged to the New York Central No. 31, a steam tugboat that was part of a large fleet operated by the New York Central Railroad. The tugboats pulled barges loaded with railroad cars across the Hudson River in the days before railway tunnels and bridges were built.

On the opposite side of the pier from the *Peking,* you'll come to the:

15. *Ambrose* **Lightship,** which was the first ship acquired by the Seaport Museum—it came to the Seaport in 1968.

Lightships lie at anchor, using lights and distinctive markings to guide ships through passages where lighthouse construction isn't feasible. The 135-foot-long *Ambrose* was built in 1908 and guided ocean liners, steamers, and other vessels through the Ambrose Channel into New York Harbor for more than 20 years.

Now move onto the next pier; the large complex you see before you is the:

16. **Pier 17 Pavilion,** an upscale shopping center overlooking the harbor. You'll find familiar names—The Limited, Campagnie Internationale Express, and The Sharper Image—along with a wide range of glitzy boutiques. The Weather Store offers a selection of umbrellas, rain slickers, and other foul-weather gear; A 2 Z and the Seaport House of Magic and Jokes are packed with toys, gag gifts, and novelties; and Pavo Real Boutique and Gallery houses huge, surreal animal sculptures and ceramics.

There's a food court for casual dining, and Liberty's Café and Oyster Bar if you opt for a full sit-down meal. Wander along the outdoor promenade surrounding the building and admire the close-up view of the Brooklyn Bridge.

Exit the Pier 17 Pavilion and turn right onto South Street. At nos. 116–119 stands:

17. **Meyer's Hotel,** the work of architect John Snook, who also designed the original Grand Central Station in 1871–72. Built in 1873, the Victorian-style hotel still boasts its original front doors with etched-glass panels and a flamboyant mirrored bar that once hosted Diamond Jim Brady and other rowdy, colorful characters.

Retrace your steps on South Street and head toward its intersection with Fulton Street, where you'll come upon the:

18. Fulton Market Building. The original market, erected in 1821, provided retail space for butchers; eventually vegetable sellers, fish merchants, and grocers set up shop there, too. As fashionable New Yorkers moved uptown in the mid-19th century, the market began to cater to wholesalers and the building fell into disrepair. It was torn down in 1880.

In 1883 a new structure was unveiled on this site—boasting not only a market, but also a telegraph office, a biological lab, and a museum that displayed "fish and animal curiosities" provided by the State Fish Commissioner.

The famous Fulton Fish Market is now across South Street, near the Pier 17 Pavilion (see Stop 1 on this tour). Inside the structure before you is a collection of pricey gourmet shops and boutiques. Here's your chance to buy fresh fish and shellfish at the Fulton Market Retail Shop, or gourmet goodies from Burke & Burke. If you wander up to the top floor, you'll come across Next Stop South Pole, a penguin boutique; Virtuality, where you can don a video helmet and experience virtual reality; and the Mark Reuben Gallery, where the vintage black-and-white prints of sports legends and of old New York make for fascinating browsing.

REFRESHMENT STOP On the mezzanine level of the Fulton Market Building is **Roebling's** (tel. 608-3980), where moderately priced fresh seafood is the order of the day. Start with New England clam chowder or half a dozen bluepoint oysters on the halfshell. All of the entrees are market fresh and subject to availability—perhaps you'll be tempted by the pan-fried crab cakes, which come with roasted pepper beurre blanc, sugar snap peas, julienne carrots, and mashed potatoes.

Across from the Fulton Market is:

19. 203 Front Street, where J. Crew offers classic clothing (including many of the same items you'll find in their famous mail-order catalog). The building itself was constructed for a grocer in 1815. Along with 204 Front Street, it was transformed in 1882–83 into a waterfront hotel catering to the many single men who earned their keep at the Seaport. The building has been restored to its 1880s appearance, including the heavily modeled storefront doors, a pressed-metal cornice, and the running-bond Philadelphia brick facade.

From Front Street, make a right onto Fulton Street. The next block off of Fulton is:

20. Water Street. At nos. 207–211 are three Greek Revival–style storefronts, built in 1835–36. Bowne & Co., Stationers, a 19th-century printing shop where you can see old equipment and techniques in action, resides at no. 211. There's a wonderful selection of cards and stationery for sale. For a fee, you can participate in hands-on workshops, perhaps printing a small book on a 19th-century letterpress or creating your own letterhead using antique type. (Reserve in advance for the workshops by calling 669-9451.)

At nos. 207–209 is the Chandlery, a Seaport Museum shop that stocks books and charts, clothing, gifts, and marine supplies. Also on this block is the Museum Gallery, where changing exhibits illustrate New York's history. You can learn more about the city's past, especially its maritime heritage, at the nearby Melville Library, a research facility that's open by appointment only.

Water, Fulton, and Pearl Streets converge at a corner that's the site of the:

21. *Titanic* **Memorial Lighthouse,** a memorial to those lost at sea when the S.S. *Titanic,* a luxury ocean liner, struck an iceberg on its maiden voyage to the United States and sank.

WALKING TOUR 3

Chinatown

Start: The intersection of Broadway and Centre Street.
Subway: Take the 6, N, or R, to Canal Street.
Finish: The intersection of East Broadway and Rutgers Street.
Time: 3 hours, not including restaurant stops.
Best Times: Sundays, when neighborhood shops and restaurants are at their most festive—and hectic.

Everyone comes to Chinatown for the food; the neighborhood's four-hundred-odd restaurants have for many years been satisfying New Yorkers' cravings for delicacies from Canton, Hunan, and Szechuan provinces (and even Vietnam and Thailand). But outside the doors of the restaurants waits the swirling, exotic streetlife of one of the largest Chinese communities in the Western Hemisphere. In the shops along Mott, Canal, and East Broadway, you'll find unusual foodstuffs, Chinese herbal medicines, and collectibles that you'd think only a trip to Hong Kong or Shanghai could net. And you can find in Chinatown's narrow streets and aging tenements the stories of the immigrants—first the English, then the Germans, Irish, Italians, Jews, and finally the Chinese—who have made this neighborhood one of their first stops in the New World.

Although East Indies trading ships brought handfuls of Chinese to New York from about 1840 on, it was not until the 1880s that Chinatown really began to develop. Thousands of Chinese sailed to

California (they called it *Gam San,* the "Gold Mountain") in the mid-19th century, hoping to amass fortunes by working the mines and building the railroads so they could return to China rich men. They were willing to work long hours for low pay, and most had little interest in learning English and assimilating American culture. By the 1870s, they became the victims of a tide of racism, violence, and legal persecution throughout the West. In 1882, Congress passed the Chinese Exclusion Act, which denied Chinese the right to citizenship, barred them from all but a handful of occupations, and suspended the immigration of Chinese laborers to the United States. Additionally, the act forbade any laborers already in the country from bringing their wives into the States. Some Chinese returned home, but tens of thousands remained and many drifted east to escape the hostile climate in the West. From 1880 to 1890 the Chinese population on Mott, Pell, and Doyers Streets increased tenfold to 12,000.

By the 1890s, Chinatown had become a large and isolated ghetto, and remained so for many years. Since World War II, however, the neighborhood has been building bridges to the American mainstream. A large influx of foreign capital from Taiwan and Hong Kong has helped make Chinatown one of New York's strongest local economies, and many Chinese Americans have joined the middle class. Come to Chinatown on a Sunday and you'll do your exploring alongside well-heeled suburbanites in for a look at the old neighborhood. But unlike other famous immigrant neighborhoods such as Little Italy or the old Lower East Side, Chinatown isn't ready to be relegated to the history books—immigrants from all around Asia continue to stream in, adding new energy and color.

A visit to Chinatown may overstimulate you—especially if you come during the raucous Chinese New Year celebrations in late January or early February—but that's not a bad price for a tantalizing experience of a people and culture from the other side of the world.

Set off to the east along Canal Street. You'll probably have to thread your way through a multiethnic throng of pedestrians and street vendors hawking toys, firecrackers, dumplings, and the like—Canal Street during business hours is one of New York's most frenzied, crowded thoroughfares. From Broadway to the Bowery, Canal Street (which is a major east-west conduit for traffic from Brooklyn over the Manhattan Bridge to New Jersey through the Holland Tunnel) is lined with bustling variety stores, fish markets, green grocers, banks, and Chinese-owned jewelry shops. Many of the storefronts have been subdivided into minimalls whose stalls purvey everything from ginseng products to martial arts paraphernalia. When night falls and the shops are shuttered, Canal Street quickly becomes almost completely deserted.

Although you'll see plenty of Chinese-language signs on Canal as soon as you walk east of Broadway, the landmark that signals your arrival in Chinatown proper is the former:

1. **Golden Pacific National Bank.** Located on the northwest corner of Canal and Centre Streets, this building was raised in 1983 as the bank's new home. At first a major point of pride in the neighborhood, the bank failed only two years later and its patrons, largely individual Chinese, lost their uninsured deposits. The building, with its pagoda roof, wild color scheme, and facade with Oriental motifs, has been resurrected as a busy jewelry exchange.

Trek five blocks east along Canal Street until you reach the Bowery. Along the way, look for a group of vegetable sellers plying their trade on a traffic island at Baxter and Canal Streets. They sell produce you'll find almost nowhere else this side of mainland China—sweet, juicy *bok choy,* or Chinese cabbage; fresh ginger, which overlays the flavor of many Chinese dishes; huge white radishes; "yard-long" green beans; and *gee choy,* a dried purple seaweed that is delicious when deep-fried or roasted. Cross from the traffic island to the southern side of Canal Street and you'll smell a briny aroma emanating from a fish market whose crushed-ice-covered displays spill well out onto the sidewalk. The aproned fish sellers keep up a steady patter, extolling the virtues of their shark, squid, snapper, oysters, and eels.

On the southwest corner of Canal Street and the Bowery is a branch of the:

2. **Manhattan Savings Bank.** With its domed roof, this is one of New York's more distinctive banks. Built in 1924, it has been overhauled and tailored to its Chinese depositors—the bank's name is inscribed in Chinese into the stone over its main portal, and the interior is decorated with Chinese-style lanterns and wallhangings.

Canal Street is lined with one bank after another; indeed, Chinatown's 150,000 residents are served by an astounding 27 banks, far more than most cities of similar size. As of 1992, combined deposits in Chinatown banks totaled $3.5 billion; much of this represents the savings of residents who work long hours at low-paying jobs six days a week and manage to put away 30%, 40%, even 50% of their wages. The thousands of new immigrants who pour into Chinatown every year are ardent pursuers of the American dream.

Across the Bowery to the east is the approach to the:

3. **Manhattan Bridge.** This suspension bridge, built in 1905, may not be the inspiration to poets and artists that the great

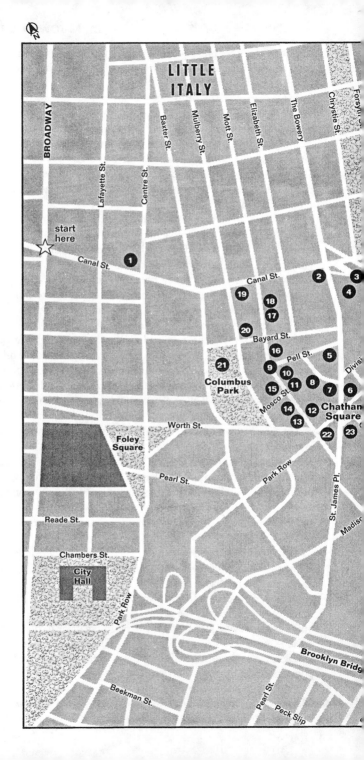

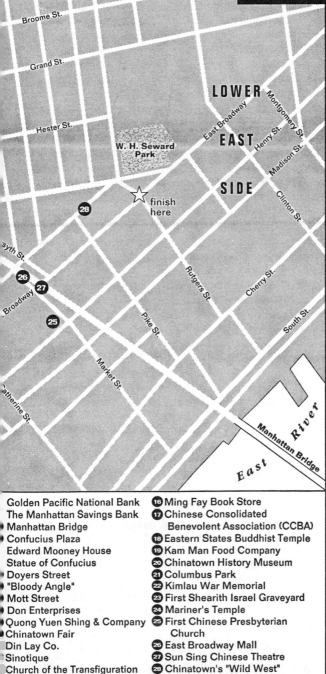

CHINATOWN

Golden Pacific National Bank
The Manhattan Savings Bank
Manhattan Bridge
Confucius Plaza
Edward Mooney House
Statue of Confucius
Doyers Street
"Bloody Angle"
Mott Street
Don Enterprises
Quong Yuen Shing & Company
Chinatown Fair
Din Lay Co.
Sinotique
Church of the Transfiguration

16 Ming Fay Book Store
17 Chinese Consolidated
   Benevolent Association (CCBA)
18 Eastern States Buddhist Temple
19 Kam Man Food Company
20 Chinatown History Museum
21 Columbus Park
22 Kimlau War Memorial
23 First Shearith Israel Graveyard
24 Mariner's Temple
25 First Chinese Presbyterian
   Church
26 East Broadway Mall
27 Sun Sing Chinese Theatre
28 Chinatown's "Wild West"

Brooklyn Bridge has been, but the monumental beaux arts colonnade and arch that stand at its entrance (in odd juxtaposition to the functional steel towers of the bridge) are quite grand and arresting.

Looming above the bridge on the east side of the Bowery is:

4. Confucius Plaza. The first major public-funded housing project built for Chinese use, Confucius Plaza extends from Division Street around to the Bowery where it rises up into a curved 43-story tower facing the entrance to the Manhattan Bridge.

The activist spirit of the 1960s touched Chinatown in a significant way; many neighborhood youths became involved in a Chinese-American pride movement that culminated in the establishment of new organizations devoted to building community centers, providing social services, and securing Chinatown a voice in city government. Winning the struggle to build Confucius Plaza and forcing contractors to hire Chinese workers showed that Chinatown was now a political heavy hitter.

Walk south on the Bowery past the mouth of Bayard Street on your right. On the southeast corner of the Bowery and Pell Street is the:

5. Edward Mooney House. This largely Georgian brick row house (painted red with yellow trim) dates from George Washington's New York days. It was built in 1785 and is the oldest such house in the city. Mooney was a wealthy meat wholesaler who snapped up this property after prominent New York tory James De Lancey abandoned it—and the new nation—after the Revolutionary War.

The Bowery reaches its southern terminus in Chatham Square, into which nine other streets converge. To your left on a traffic island you'll see the:

6. Statue of Confucius. Built in 1976 to complement the Confucius Plaza development, this bronze statue and its green marble base were a gift of the Chinese Consolidated Benevolent Association (CCBA), which has served as Chinatown's unofficial government for over a hundred years. The organization has always represented conservative Chinese who support traditional notions of family loyalty and respect for one's elders and leaders; the statue was built over the strenuous objections of activist groups that felt the neighborhood should display a more progressive cultural symbol. However, the sage's 2,400-year-old words, inscribed in the monument's base in both Chinese and English, are strikingly descriptive of the strength of Chinatown's tight-knit social fabric: Confucius recommends that we look beyond our immediate family and see *all* our elders as our parents, and all children as our own.

Look just south of the Confucius statue and you'll see another branch of the Manhattan Savings Bank, this one with the traditional Chinese pagoda-style roof and gold trim.

From the statue of Confucius, follow Catherine Street past the bank (which flanks the street's right side), then turn left onto East Broadway. This thoroughfare is now the heart of commercial, workaday Chinatown. Very few of its businesses are oriented toward tourists; instead, they are dedicated to serving the Chinese community's needs. There are Chinese video stores, beauty salons, sidewalk shacks purveying grilled meats and dumplings, and bakeries whose wedding cakes come complete with figurines of bride and groom with Asian features.

REFRESHMENT STOPS A Chinatown tradition that brings out the gourmand in everyone, *dim sum* (Cantonese for "dot your heart") presents you with one small gastronomic delight after another until you can eat no more. Every day from about 9am to 4pm, two huge, showy East Broadway restaurants, the **Golden Unicorn** at 18 East Broadway (tel. 941-0911) and the **Nice Restaurant** at 35 East Broadway (tel. 406-9510) draw hungry crowds. The Golden Unicorn's walkie-talkie–wielding hostess directs incoming diners to the restaurant's second- and third-floor dining rooms, whereas in the Nice Restaurant, the lobby has several tanks full of carp and sea bass. Often you'll be asked to sit with other parties around a huge banquet table. Once you're settled, you'll see that there's a distinctly celebratory spirit pervading these swank dining rooms; the Chinese families dining here always seem to have three or four generations represented when they go out for a meal.

You'll be presented with a pot of tea and a moist hot towel with which to clean your hands. Then let the feast begin: Simply choose what looks appealing from the carts that waitresses trundle around the room. You can afford to take some risks—everything costs between $2 and $4 a portion (the waitress will mark your check every time you select a new dish). Some of the best dishes at the Nice Restaurant are the B.B.Q pork buns (sweet chewy buns filled with tangy pieces of barbecued pork) and the "farinaceous" shrimp rolls—big, tasty shrimp wrapped in a wide, slick rice noodle and covered with soy sauce. The Golden Unicorn's winners include shark fin dumplings and delicately sweet lotus seed sesame balls.

Backtrack to Chatham Square. At the mouth of the Bowery on the square, a narrow, crooked street bears off to the northwest. This is:

7. Doyers Street, which along with Pell Street and the lower end of Mott Street formed the original Chinatown. Doyers was the backdrop for much of the neighborhood's unhappy early history.

Chinatown's "bachelor society," which existed from 1882 to 1943 (when some provisions of the Exclusion Act were repealed), was a place of grimly limited opportunity and deep poverty. There were 27 men to every woman in the neighborhood. Prohibited from competing with whites for work, and hemmed into Chinatown by the language barrier and even the risk of being beaten if they strayed from the three-block ghetto, most of the men eked out a living in the laundry industry.

Crime compounded the neighborhood's misery. The Chinese moved into the northern end of an area that for 40 years had been a sprawling morass of saloons, gambling dens, and squalid tenements extending from Chatham Square all the way to the waterfront. The CCBA acted as de facto government, but real power resided in the *tongs,* protection societies involved in racketeering and gambling. There are still tong-controlled gaming dens in Chinatown, still whispers of intimidation and an occasional outbreak of gang-related violence.

The post office located a few paces up Doyers Street on your right now occupies the site of the old Chatham Club, one of the uproarious music halls that surrounded Chatham Square a century ago. The clubs boasted singing waiters, accompanied by a tinny piano, who would entertain the clientele with sentimental ballads. Both Izzy Baline and Al Yoelson sang at the Chatham and other clubs on Doyers; in tonier surroundings, they later became better known as Irving Berlin and Al Jolson.

By the 1920s, the sharp bend in Doyers Street had acquired its reputation as the infamous:

8. "Bloody Angle." The first two tongs to rise in Chinatown, the On Leong and the Hip Sing, engaged in a fierce struggle for turf and precedence in Chinatown that dragged on for almost 40 years. Both organizations had large "standing armies" of henchmen, and the worst of the bloodshed between the two tongs occurred here—the crooked street lent itself to ambush, and assassins could usually make a fast escape by ducking through the old Chinese Theatre, which stood right in the elbow of the street, that the New Vietnam restaurant now occupies. At the turn of the century, Bloody Angle was the site of more murders than anywhere else in the United States.

As lawless as "bachelor society" Chinatown could be, the reality always paled in comparison to the lurid portraits of the community retailed by the newspapers and tour guides. The most notorious of the tour guides was one Chuck Connors. A gifted storyteller, he translated his familiarity with the Cantonese dialect and his willingness to take license with the truth into celebrity among the New York socialites he would escort through the neighborhood. Connors never hesitated to point to any man walking down the street and label him a hatchetman for the tongs or an opium addict; his baroque finale was a fake opium den, complete with a man and woman posing as opium addict and "white slave girl." Such fictions satisfied the sensation-seekers of that time, but had little in common with the day-to-day existence of almost all of Chinatown's men.

At the end of Doyers is Pell Street, another short, narrow thoroughfare that has changed little over the years; it's lined with venerable restaurants such as Pell's Dinty and the Bo-Bo Restaurant. At no. 16 is the unobtrusive entryway to the headquarters of the organization that has dominated Pell and Doyers Streets for a hundred years, the Hip Sing tong.

Leaving the dark side of the neighborhood's history behind, walk west on Pell to its intersection with:

9. Mott Street, the heart of old Chinatown. Mott is the epicenter of the tumultuous Chinese New Year celebrations that begin with the first full moon after January 21. For weeks beforehand, shops all through Chinatown do a booming business as residents stock up for their holiday feasts, purchase presents for friends and family, and buy New Year's bells, firecrackers, lucky lotus seeds and birds, and calendars. Red and gold streamers festoon every shop window and interior, hang over every street, and brighten every home at New Year's. When the big day arrives, one of New York's most chaotic and colorful street parties begins, featuring parades complete with gyrating dragon dancers and a nonstop thunder of firecrackers.

The shops that line Mott Street are a diverse bunch, and collectively their stock will surely give you the chance to bring a piece of Chinatown back home with you. Just around the corner to your left is one such store:

10. Don Enterprises, at 36 Mott Street. This shop is chock full of interesting lamps and ornate figurines of the sages and emperors of eons ago, but the best reason to enter is to have a look at the store's gargantuan ceramic urns and to talk to the friendly clerks.

A few doors down is:

11. Quong Yuen Shing & Company, at 32 Mott Street. The oldest store in Chinatown, Quong Yuen Shing celebrated its 100th birthday in 1991. It has changed remarkably little—the tin ceiling, hanging scales, and the decorative panels in the back above the counter (over which Chinese herbal medicines were dispensed) all keep the place looking just as it did in the 1890s. Along with sandalwood fans, tea and mah-jongg sets, various ceramic bowls and vases, and seeds for all those mysterious-looking Chinese vegetables on sale in the streets, the store still sells merchandise it's been stocking for a century. One such item are silk handkerchiefs, which Chinatown laundries would buy and pass on to their best customers at Christmastime.

Make your way down to the:

12. Chinatown Fair, at 8 Mott Street. From the outside this place looks like just another video arcade, but tucked in between the familiar machines are vintage pinball games and other arcade antiques like the Luv-O-Meter, the Arm Pull, and a photobooth. Two glass-enclosed booths house live performing chickens—one is a master of tic-tac-toe and the other dances. A sign above the dancer's booth advises that how well she performs "depends on her mood." Five minutes here and you'll half expect to spot the gleaming red eyes of a Zoltan machine (like the one that sent Tom Hanks for a loop in the movie *Big*).

Across Mott is the:

13. Din Lay Co., at 5 Mott Street. An old, slightly musty shop, Din Lay is worth a visit for its unbeatable collection of classic Chinatown souvenirs—there are mah-jongg sets and tables, incense burners, joss sticks, tea sets, delicate sandalwood and rice-paper fans, sandalwood-scented soap, stainless-steel balls to roll in your hand to improve your strength and coordination, and, last but not least, Tiger Balm, which purports to soothe "overheated" skin.

A few doors up to the north is:

14. Sinotique, at 19a Mott Street. Inside this refined, decidedly upscale shop you'll find beautiful Chinese antiques, crafts, and collectibles. My favorites included rosewood and teak cabinets with delicate hand-carved ornamentation, tasteful framed Buddhist watercolors, "no-glaze" pottery made with four-thousand-year-old methods, and hand-wrought-mounted bronze gongs. New Age Chinese music circulates through the shop—if you like it, you can take home a CD.

Cross tiny Mosco Street (named for a prominent Little Italy pol) and you'll be in front of the:

15. Church of the Transfiguration, at 25–29 Mott Street. This Georgian church with a number of traceried Gothic windows was built in 1801; the spire was added in the 1860s. Originally consecrated as the English Lutheran First Church of Zion, Transfiguration has remade itself in the changing image of the neighborhood many times, first as a house of worship for English Lutherans, and then, after it was reconsecrated as a Catholic church, serving the newly arrived Irish, and later, in the 1880s, the Italians. You can still hear an English mass at Transfiguration, but nowadays its Cantonese and Mandarin services draw by far the greater crowds—the church is the focal point of New York's Chinese Roman Catholic community. Transfiguration remains true to its heritage as a mission house, continuing to offer English classes and other services that help its members find their way into the American mainstream.

REFRESHMENT STOP Just north of the Church of the Transfiguration is the **New Lung Fong Bakery,** 41 Mott Street (tel. 233-7447). Chinese bakeries offer unusual, moderately sweet treats such as red-bean cake, lotus seed pastry, and sticky rice cake. Sitting in Lung Fong's unadorned café section, you can relax with a cup of tea or coffee and *yum cha*—that's Chinese for hanging out, talking and drinking, in a café. All of Lung Fong's pastry is marked with English labels.

Continue walking north on Mott. Across the street at 42 Mott Street is the:

16. **Ming Fay Book Store.** An eclectic store with everything from Zippo lighters and toys to Chinese-language calendars, newspapers, comics, pinup magazines, and books, Ming Fay also carries an interesting selection of English-language books on Chinese subjects. A sampling of titles: *Chinese Astrology, Bruce Lee's Fighting Method, Chinese Idioms, The ABC of Traditional Chinese Medicine,* and *The Living Buddha.*

Just past the bookstore on your right is a permanent food stall that sells nothing but fried white-radish cakes, and a little farther up Mott at no. 62 is the headquarters of the:

17. **Chinese Consolidated Benevolent Association (CCBA).** Until fairly recently, it functioned as the working government of Chinatown, helping new immigrants find jobs and housing, funneling capital into neighborhood businesses, offering English classes to children and adults, providing services to the elderly, and even operating criminal courts. While its influence has waned somewhat, it is still a major social and political force in Chinatown, and is the voice of New York's pro-Taiwan community. Also located in the building is the

Chinese School, which since 1915 has been working to keep the Chinese traditions and language alive, long a primary concern of the CCBA.

Right next door is the:

18. Eastern States Buddhist Temple. This storefront shrine has been here for years. Quiet and suffused with incense, the temple seems to serve as something of a social center—there are always a number of elderly women sitting in the chairs that line the wall. You can enter, light a joss stick, and perhaps offer a prayer to Kuan Yin, the Chinese goddess of mercy.

Across the street at the corner of Mott and Canal, behind a stately facade that includes balconies and a pagoda roof, is the headquarters of the Chinese Merchants Association, better known as On Leong. It is Chinatown's oldest tong, and still one of most prominent neighborhood organizations.

Take a left onto Canal Street. A steady stream of shoppers will no doubt be passing in and out of the:

19. Kam Man Food Company, at 200 Canal Street. The king of Chinese supermarkets, Kam Man is a fascinating place to explore. To your right, as you enter the store is a selection of elaborately packaged teas and elixirs laced with ginseng and other mainstays of the Chinese pharmacopoeia—look for Essence of Chicken and Vitality Tea for Men (which promises great potency). Just beyond this collection is a counter underneath which all variety of domestic and Korean ginseng root are on display for what to you may seem like astonishing prices. Walk toward the rear of the store and you'll find packages of *dim sum* buns ready for the steamer or the wok. The center of the main floor is devoted to dried and prepared foods of astonishing variety: There are piles of preserved squid and skate, salted fish, packages of dried oysters and shrimp, nuts of all kinds, and great glass containers of dried mushrooms. Downstairs you'll find teas, cookery, sweets like preserved plums and tamarind candy, roasted seaweed, and literally oodles of noodles. On the landing between floors are displayed health beverages ranging from "lung tonic" to medicinal teas that promise to "revigorate" you. After a short while, all the unrecognizable delicacies become the norm, and it's the odd jar of mayonnaise or box of baking powder that really looks strange.

Turn left onto Mulberry and walk down to the:

20. Chinatown History Museum, at 70 Mott Street (second floor, entrance on Bayard Street). In the forward-looking, upwardly mobile climate of today's Chinatown, not many want to think about the cruel hardships that the first generations of Chinese in New York suffered. This museum, founded in 1980, has taken on the important responsibility of serving as the neighborhood's official memory. The curators have painstakingly collected memorabilia and, more important, stories from those who emigrated from China to live here in the early years of this century.

The museum's wonderful permanent exhibition, "Remembering New York Chinatown," combines these elements into an evocative story of the Chinese-American experience. The exhibit also encourages Chinese visitors to add their recollections to the museum's archives. Visitors hungry for more information on specific topics can consult the Resource Bank, an excellent pool of information on the garment and restaurant industries and other economic mainstays of Chinatown, the tongs, Chuck Connors, and many other subjects. An adjoining gallery stages temporary exhibitions of work by Chinese artists and photographers.

Opening off to the southwest on the other side of Mulberry Street is:

21. Columbus Park. Open public spaces are in short supply on the Lower East Side of Manhattan, and Columbus Park is popular with Chinatown residents both young and old. The park lies where a huddle of decrepit tenements known as Mulberry Bend once stood. In the last quarter of the 19th century, Mulberry Bend was New York's very worst slum, as evinced by the frightening nomenclature it acquired—the filthy rookeries went by names such as Bone Alley, Kerosene Row, and Bandits' Roost. Such brawling street gangs as the Dead Rabbits, Plug Uglies, and Whyos were the powers of Mulberry Bend, and police would only venture into the area in platoons of 10 or more. Mulberry Bend remained New York's disgrace until social reformer Jacob Riis managed to work public ire up to the point where city officials were obliged to raze the slum from 1892 to 1894. For the last century, Riis's vision of a clean place for neighborhood children to play has been made a reality— there are almost always pick-up basketball or street-hockey games in progress in the park.

At the southern end of the park, make a left turn onto Worth Street and you'll soon be back at Chatham Square. On the near traffic island is the.

22. Kimlau War Memorial, built in 1962 to honor the Chinese Americans who gave their lives while serving in the U.S. armed forces. Chinatown's extraordinary contribution to the American war effort in World War II—40% of the neighborhood's population served in the military—was a major factor in the annulment of the Chinese Exclusion Act and other anti-Chinese legislation.

St. James Street, which extends south from Chatham Square, is the site of the:

23. **First Shearith Israel Graveyard,** a burial ground for the Sephardic Jews who emigrated to New York in the mid-17th century. The 1683 stone of Benjamin Bueno de Mesquita is the oldest in the city; the cemetery remained active until 1828 and features the graves of a number of soldiers who died during the American Revolution.

Backtrack on St. James Street and turn right onto Oliver Street. On the northeast corner of Oliver and Henry Streets is the:

24. **Mariner's Temple.** This Greek Revival brownstone church, with an entryway fronted by two Ionic columns, was built in 1844. Today, a Baptist church serving a mixed Chinese, African-American, and Latino congregation, the Mariner's Temple originally catered to the sea captains, dockworkers, and sailors of the sprawling maritime community that dominated the waterfront along the East River in the 19th century.

Two blocks east on Henry Street is the:

25. **First Chinese Presbyterian Church,** which shares a place in neighborhood history with the Mariner's Temple. Built in 1819 on the outskirts of the Cherry Hill section (which after the Revolutionary War was New York's poshest neighborhood and the site of the nation's first presidential mansion), this Georgian-style house of worship was originally named the Northeast Dutch Reformed Church. It was renamed the Church of Sea and Land during the mid-19th century, when the East River water-front had become rife with cutthroat saloons, dance halls, and "crimps"—lodging houses that often took advantage of their sailor patrons by robbing them or even "shanghaiing" them aboard outgoing ships. Mission houses like the Mariner's Temple and the Church of Sea and Land were often the only place to which beleaguered seafarers and immigrants could turn for help. Today, the church continues to assist the immigrants that arrive in Chinatown in droves every year.

Turn left and follow Market Street to bustling East Broadway. As unlikely as this may seem, the dim, noisy area underneath the Manhattan Bridge is the current commercial hot spot of Chinatown. You'll see on your left the:

26. **East Broadway Mall,** a place that may cause you to wonder if you're actually in Hong Kong. The stores cater entirely to Chinese shoppers and include a newsstand at which you'll be lucky to spot a word of English, a shop selling Chinese pop music, two Chinese-language video stores, several beauty salons and cosmetics shops selling products you won't find in your average health and beauty aids store, and Ho's Ginseng Co.,

where you can get something to cool down your blood (or warm it up). The mall's centerpiece is a glitzy new restaurant, the Triple Eight Palace, serving Hong Kong–style cuisine—Hong Kong cooking (essentially a more elegant, international version of Cantonese) is the culinary rage in Chinatown nowadays.

Facing the East Broadway Mall under the bridge is the:

27. Sun Sing Chinese Theatre. Once Chinatown's opera house, Sun Sing has been strictly a movie theater since 1950. Most of the Hong Kong films presented here have subtitles, but it hardly matters with kung fu epics and action-adventures like *Once Upon a Time in China* or *God of Gambling;* the sappy romances and melodramas that sometimes share the bill are just as easy to follow.

Continue along East Broadway, and you'll soon cross Pike Street. Pike is an unofficial divider between establishment Chinatown and an expanding area that's been termed:

28. Chinatown's "Wild West" by journalist Gwen Kinkead in her book *Chinatown: A Portrait of a Closed Society* (Harper Collins, 1992). Asians have been flooding into New York City ever since U.S. immigration laws were liberalized in 1965. The great majority of them hail from the People's Republic of China, and most of these new immigrants come from Fujian Province, often via Hong Kong or Taiwan. These new arrivals have almost completely replaced the old immigrant residents of the Lower East Side, the Jews. Emblematic of the changing makeup in the neighborhood is the **Sons of Israel Kalwarie Synagogue,** located just down Pike Street to the right of East Broadway. It now stands abandoned and boarded up like many of the Lower East Side's Jewish landmarks.

Just beyond Pike Street at 125 East Broadway you'll see the twin stone lions and green pagoda roof surrounding the entrance of the **Fukien American Association.** It is one of several Fujianese organizations that are competing with old Chinatown's established tongs for turf in this new frontier; friction between the tongs has become fairly commonplace.

Walk down East Broadway to Rutgers Street (where you'll find the entrance to the subway's East Broadway F-line stop). The Chinatown you'll pass on your way may have no fancy restaurants, curio shops, or pagoda roofs, but no storefront here stands empty. The barber shops, fish markets, and newsstands here may look as though they've been built on a wing and a prayer, but they do a brisk business. Many of the buildings you pass house small garment factories just like the sweatshops in which Jewish laborers worked for their family's future on East Broadway 75 years ago. You'll find around you the hectic commerce, the hardworking laborers, the neatly dressed schoolchildren, the hum of a neighborhood whose people will soon be leaving these gritty streets on their way into the mainstream, just as people on the Lower East Side have been doing for more than a century.

WALKING TOUR 4

The Jewish Lower East Side

Start: The Henry Street Settlement, 263–267 Henry Street.
Subway: Take the F to East Broadway and Rutgers Street; walk south on Rutgers and make a left on Henry Street.
Finish: Russ and Daughters, 179 East Houston Street.
Time: Approximately 3 to 4 hours.
Best Times: Sundays, when you can tour Schapiro's and the Eldridge Street Synagogue and see Orchard Street in full hubbub. If you begin about 9:30am, you'll get a chance to look inside Bialystoker Synagogue.
Worst Times: Saturdays and Jewish holidays, when almost everything is closed; Friday afternoons, when stores close early.

The Lower East Side has always been one of New York's most colorful neighborhoods. Over 23 million Europeans emigrated to American shores between 1880 and 1919, seeking escape from famine, poverty, and religious persecution. About 1.5 million Jews—many of them fleeing Russian pogroms—wound up in ramshackle tenements here. They scratched out a meager livelihood peddling wares on Orchard Street or working dawn to dusk in garment center sweatshops. By 1920, some five hundred synagogues and religious schools (talmud torahs) dotted the area. Though the garment center has moved uptown, and the ethnic mix is different today, Orchard Street—the area's primary shopping artery—and its immediate surroundings remain a largely Orthodox Jewish enclave. And the area is rich in Jewish history. Don't eat much before starting out; there's great noshing along the way.

Our first stop is the:

1. The Henry Street Settlement, 263–267 Henry Street. Called to tend a patient on Ludlow Street in 1892, 25-year-old German-Jewish nurse Lillian Wald was appalled at the squalor of tenement life. She moved downtown in order to study conditions in the Jewish ghetto, and, in 1893, established a district nursing service on Henry Street. Two years later, it evolved into the Henry Street Settlement, one of America's first social agencies, offering job training, educational facilities, activities and summer camps for children, concerts, and plays. German-Jewish philanthropist Jacob Schiff donated the three Henry Street buildings you see before you.

Wald dedicated her life to helping the indigent of the Lower East Side fight disease, malnutrition, and ignorance, and the "house on Henry Street" initiated progressive social legislation, including child labor laws. Social reformer Jacob Riis said of her, "From the very start, the poor became 'her people.' She took them to her heart and they quickly gave her unstinted love and trust . . ." Years ago you might have seen Jane Addams, Albert Einstein, or Eleanor Roosevelt discussing vital social issues in the dining room. More recently, President Bill Clinton visited during his 1992 campaign. The settlement continues its good works, operating homeless shelters and numerous other programs for neighborhood residents. Its three original late-Federal buildings, today used only for administrative purposes, are designated landmarks.

Make a right on Montgomery Street, and bear right to Samuel Dickstein Place. Across Grand Street is:

2. The Louis Abrons Arts Center/Harry De Jur Henry Street Settlement Playhouse, 466 Grand Street. Founded by sisters Alice and Irene Lewisohn in 1915 to stage productions of the Henry Street Settlement's youthful dramatic groups, this renowned center went on to present premieres of S. Ansky's *The Dybbuk* (attended by authors Edna Ferber and Willa Cather) and James Joyce's *Exiles,* along with plays by George Bernard Shaw, Havelock Ellis, Anton Chekhov, Scholem Asch, and Eugene O'Neill. It remains a vital performance space and cultural center, offering a comprehensive schedule of dance, theater, music, art exhibits, classes, and workshops. Pick up an events schedule while you're here. The center is housed in a three-story Georgian Revival building with a newer adjacent extension.

Around the corner on Willett Street is the:

3. **Bialystoker Synagogue,** 7 Bialystoker Place (Willett Street). Occupying a converted 1826 fieldstone church with a pedimented facade, this beautiful Orthodox landsmanschaft shul (synagogue of countrymen) was purchased in 1905 by an immigrant congregation from Bialystok (then in Russia, today in Poland). The congregation itself was organized in 1878, and, in honor of its 100th anniversary, Willett Street was renamed Bialystoker Place in 1978. The temple's interior walls are ornately painted with Moorish motifs, zodiac signs (which are found in the Jewish Scriptural interpretations of the cabala), and biblical scenes such as the Wailing Wall and the burial place of Rachel. The gold-leafed ark, designed in Italy, is embellished with lions and eagles. And glittering crystal chandeliers are suspended from a ceiling painted as a blue sky with fluffy white clouds.

Bialystoker Synagogue is open on Sundays until about 10:30am (there are services from 6:15 to 10am); if you're going at another time, you can call a day or two ahead (tel. 475-0165) to arrange admission.

Return to Grand Street and make a right, then make a left on Clinton Street, and a right on East Broadway to the:

4. **Educational Alliance,** 197 East Broadway. The Alliance was founded in 1889 by "uptown" German-Jewish philanthropists to help fellow immigrants assimilate, Americanize, and adapt to a baffling alien culture. It offered them training in English, courses in business, cultural and civic programs, legal counsel, music lessons, and athletic facilities, not to mention such hard-to-come-by amenities as hot showers and pasteurized milk for children. Here pre-school youngsters attended enrichment programs to prepare them for public school, a forerunner of the Head Start program of the 1960s. Immigrants learned about American history, celebrated new holidays like July Fourth and Lincoln's birthday, and attended lectures on everything from American literature to philosophy.

Today, the Educational Alliance's programs operate out of 21 locations and serve not only Jews, but black, Chinese, and Latin American New Yorkers. A Hall of Fame on the main floor is lined with photos of notable alumni such as Eddie Cantor, David Sarnoff, Jan Peerce, Jacob Epstein, Arthur Murray, and Louise Nevelson.

Continue in the same direction to:

5. **The Forward Building,** 175 East Broadway. For 60 years, this was the home of America's most prominent Yiddish newspaper—one of over 150 such papers published around the turn of the century. Founded in 1897 by a group of Russian Jewish

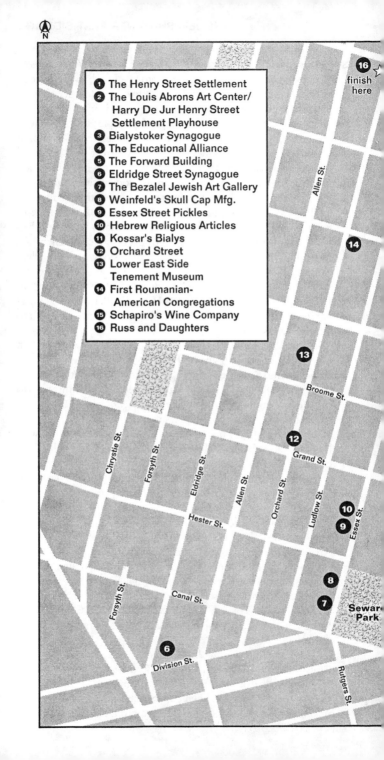

N

① The Henry Street Settlement
② The Louis Abrons Art Center/
   Harry De Jur Henry Street
   Settlement Playhouse
③ Bialystoker Synagogue
④ The Educational Alliance
⑤ The Forward Building
⑥ Eldridge Street Synagogue
⑦ The Bezalel Jewish Art Gallery
⑧ Weinfeld's Skull Cap Mfg.
⑨ Essex Street Pickles
⑩ Hebrew Religious Articles
⑪ Kossar's Bialys
⑫ Orchard Street
⑬ Lower East Side
   Tenement Museum
⑭ First Roumanian-
   American Congregations
⑮ Schapiro's Wine Company
⑯ Russ and Daughters

⑯ finish here

Allen St.

⑭

⑬

Broome St.

⑫ Grand St.

Chrystie St.
Forsyth St.
Eldridge St.
Allen St.
Orchard St.
Ludlow St.
Essex St.

⑩
⑨

Hester St.

⑧
⑦

Seward Park

Forsyth St.
Canal St.

⑥
Division St.

Rutgers St.

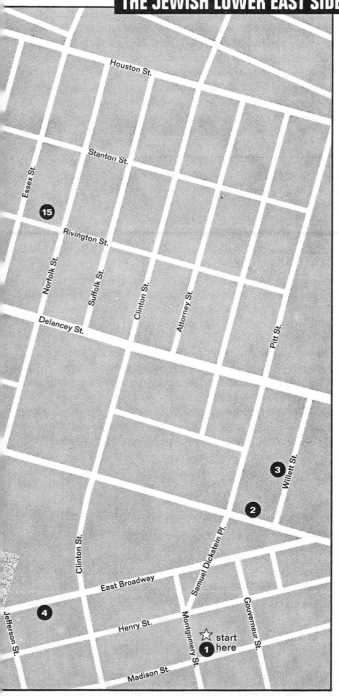

THE JEWISH LOWER EAST SIDE

Houston St.

Stanton St.

Essex St.

15

Rivington St.

Norfolk St.

Suffolk St.

Clinton St.

Attorney St.

Pitt St.

Delancey St.

Willett St.

3

2

Clinton St.

East Broadway

Samuel Dickstein Pl.

Gouverneur St.

4

Jefferson St.

Henry St.

Montgomery St.

☆ start here

1

Madison St.

immigrants, the *"Forverts"* guided thousands of Eastern European Jews through the confusing maze of American society. In the 1920s, its circulation was 250,000 copies a day.

Lithuanian immigrant Abraham Cahan served as editor from the newspaper's inception until his death in 1951. Under his inspired guidance, this socialist and zealously pro-labor newspaper examined every facet of Jewish and American life. It explained American customs and social graces to greenhorns—everything from baseball to personal hygiene—and exhorted readers to learn English and educate their children. Readers could air their problems in the New World in a column called the Bintel Brief (Bundle of Letters)—an immigrant version of Ann Landers. And the paper presented—along with trashy serialized romance novels—quality fiction by writers like Sholom Asch, Sholom Aleichem, I. J. Singer, and I. B. Singer. I. B. Singer worked on staff throughout his adult life, and all his books were written in Yiddish (later translated) and published first in *The Forward*.

Today the Forward building, constructed in 1912 specifically to house the paper, is owned by a Chinese-American organization. The flaming torches (socialist symbols) and portraits of Marx and Engels on its facade are obscured by Chinese signage. But *The Forward* is still a vital newspaper headquartered uptown. Since 1990, it has published in English as well as in Yiddish. You can buy a copy at most Manhattan newsstands.

Make a right on Rutgers Street, a left on Division Street, and a right on Eldridge Street to the:

6. **Eldridge Street Synagogue,** 12–16 Eldridge Street. The synagogue was built in 1886 by a congregation of Polish and Russian Jews; it was the most magnificent of the Lower East Side's temples. It was also the first synagogue built by Eastern European immigrants, who had previously worshiped in converted churches. Its architectural and interior decor blended Gothic and Romanesque styles with Moorish touches (flamboyant Oriental motifs were popular in mid- to late-19th-century synagogue architecture). The opulent sanctuary—under a 70-foot central dome—was fitted out with Victorian glass-shaded brass chandeliers (suspended from an elaborately painted barrel-vaulted ceiling), an ornately carved towering walnut ark from Italy, trompe l'oeil murals, exquisite stained-glass windows, and scagliola columns. And the grandiose terra-cotta and brick facade was highly symbolic in conception, its cluster of five small windows representing the five books of Moses, the 12 roundels of the rose window the twelve tribes of Israel, and so on.

The congregation flourished for several decades, but as

wealthy members moved away from the Lower East Side—and quota laws of the 1920s slowed new immigration to a trickle—funds became short, and the building deteriorated. The Depression years exacerbated the synagogue's financial difficulties, and by the 1940s the main sanctuary was in such bad repair that it was boarded up. It wasn't until the late 1970s that urban preservationists and historians began taking an interest in the synagogue. In the mid-1980s, the Eldridge Street Project got underway, restoring and preserving this historic edifice—today a designated landmark. Today, the premises are being restored as an active synagogue and a Jewish heritage center. Visitors can take one-hour tours every Sunday on the hour from noon to 4pm (other days by appointment). Admission is charged; it goes to the very worthy cause of continuing the renovation.

Make a right on Canal Street (ahead) and a left on Essex Street, where you'll find many fascinating little shops carrying Judaica and religious articles.

7. The Bezalel Jewish Art Gallery, 11 Essex Street (upstairs), is worth a look. Run by a Hungarian couple, Olga Berkowitz and Moshe Weinstock, it displays Olga's paintings along with works by Israeli and American Jewish artists, along with antique prints and beautifully decorated *ketubahs* (Jewish marriage contracts).

Also of interest on this block is:

8. Weinfeld's Skull Cap Mfg., 19 Essex Street, a century-old yarmulke factory run by succeeding generations of Weinfelds. They also make tallith (fringed prayer shawls worn by men during Jewish religious services, as are yarmulkes) and tallith bags here.

Continue uptown toward:

9. Essex Street Pickles (better known as Guss Pickle Products), 35 Essex Street, which was featured in the movie *Crossing Delancey*. An outdated sign over the awning proclaims: "Three generations of quality; please keep hands out of barrels." Guss's originated in 1910, and it's now in the fourth generation. Said barrels are filled with sours, half sours, hot pickles, pickled tomatoes, olives, sauerkraut, and other delicacies. Everything is made on the premises. Buy a delicious pickle to eat on the street, or purchase a jar full.

Just up the block is:

10. Hebrew Religious Articles, at 45 Essex Street. The shop has been here for over 50 years. Its shelves and display cases are cluttered with Jewish books, ritual phylacteries and shawls, sacred scrolls, commentaries on the Torah, menorahs, antique Judaica, electric memorial candles, seder plates, mezuzahs, yarmulkes, and a marvelous collection of turn-of-the-century Eastern European postcards.

Make a right on Grand Street to:

11. **Kossar's Bialys,** 367 Grand Street, where you can watch bakers making bialys, bagels, and *bulkas* (long bialylike rolls). Bialys were invented by bakers from the Polish town of Bialystok, and this shop has been making them since the turn of the century. Buy some oven-fresh breads to take home.

Now walk west on Grand Street and make a right into:

12. **Orchard Street.** It's hard to imagine, but Orchard Street was named for the orchards of an 18th-century farm at this location. In the 19th century, it was a vast outdoor marketplace, with rows of pushcarts lining both sides of the street. It was picturesque (though I'm sure no one thought so at the time) and vastly unsanitary. Today, pushcarts have been replaced by stores, though much of the merchandise is still displayed outside on racks. This is bargain shopping. You can save up to 50% over uptown department stores here, and many shop owners are willing to haggle over prices. (However, don't expect polite service.) Sundays the street is so jammed with shoppers that it is closed to vehicular traffic between Delancey and Houston Streets. But Orchard Street on Sunday is a phenomenon you must experience at least once. Come back to do serious shopping on a weekday when you have the stores to yourself.

Between Broome and Delancey Streets you'll come to the:

13. **Lower East Side Tenement Museum,** 97 Orchard Street (tel. 431-0233). Appropriately housed in an 1863 six-story tenement, this unique museum documents the lives of its immigrant residents. Over 10,000 people from 20 different countries lived here over a period of 72 years. I daresay these immigrants would have been astonished to hear that their crowded building of cold, cramped apartments would one day be listed on the National Register of Historic Places. A genealogist has collected the names of over a thousand past tenants, which you can check for names of your own forebears.

You can view a two-sided dollhouselike model of the building that shows how it looked in 1870—including tenants and furnishings—and in 1915. Residents lived in three-room apartments with a total area of just 325 square feet! Scant light trickled through windows at distant ends of railroad flats (they faced another line of tenements), and the only heat came from the coal- or wood-burning stove that was also used for cooking. Large families, often supplemented by boarders for the extra cash, lived in such dwellings without hot water or electricity. Toilets were in the hall. By 1915, as many as 18 people sometimes occupied one apartment, sleeping in shifts. In such unhealthy conditions, 40% of the babies born here died (according to 1900 census figures), and disease was rampant. There are photographs and artifacts on display. Future plans call for the re-creation of two actual apartments, one from 1880, another from the Depression era.

The museum is open Tuesday to Friday from 11am to 4pm, on Sundays from 10am to 5pm. Admission is free; donations are appreciated. Pick up a schedule of the museum's Sunday neighborhood tours for future excursions.

REFRESHMENT STOP Ratner's Dairy Restaurant, 138 Delancey, between Norfolk and Suffolk Streets (tel. 677-5588), is the oldest Jewish dairy restaurant in the city. People have been coming here for blintzes, borscht, gefilte fish, and matzo brei since 1917. Former New York Governor Nelson Rockefeller always ate here the night before elections (he said it was good luck). All breads and cakes are baked on the premises, so a basket of scrumptious onion rolls accompanies every meal, and there are great desserts (try the strawberry cheesecake). Open Sunday to Thursday from 6am to 11pm, Fridays from 6am to 3pm, and Saturdays from sundown to 1am.

Continue uptown, past Delancey Street, to Rivington Street, where you'll make a right to reach:

14. First Roumanian-American Congregation, *Shaarai Shamoyim* (Gates of Heaven), at 89 Rivington Street. An Orthodox congregation bought this Romanesque Revival building, formerly a Methodist church, in 1890. Two of its esteemed cantors—Richard Tucker and Jan Peerce—went on to operatic acclaim. Today, the building is sadly run down.

Continue east to:

15. Schapiro's Wine Company, 126 Rivington Street. New York City's only winery, operated by three generations of the Schapiro family, has been making kosher wines for religious and secular purposes since 1899. Its founder, the present owner's grandfather, also operated a restaurant on Attorney Street, where he used to give new immigrants a free meal, a bottle of honey wine, and 50¢. Free 15-minute tours are given on the hour Sundays between 11am and 4pm, but you can always sample some of the 29 varieties, which include wines made from honey, plums, blackberries, and New York State grapes, as well as French and California kosher wines. The grapes are harvested and crushed under rabbinical supervision during the months of September and October and stored in five-thousand-gallon redwood vats on the premises. After fermentation and filtering, the wine is boiled, aged in oak casks, and bottled. Only Sabbath-observant Orthodox Jews are allowed to handle the wine in preparation. Schapiro's concord and malaga are heavy and sweet in the Jewish tradition, advertised as "wine you can almost cut with a knife." Cellar walls are hung with photographs of the Lower East Side at the turn of the century. Schapiro's is open Monday to Friday from 10am to 5pm, and Sundays from 11am to 4pm.

Walk back to Orchard Street and continue north to Houston Street.

REFRESHMENT STOP **Katz's Delicatessen,** 205 East Houston Street, at Ludlow Street (tel. 254-2246), is a classic New York deli that's been in business at this location since 1889. The interior is little changed from those days. Even the World War II sign reading "Send a salami to your boy in the Army" is still intact. Katz's was the setting for Meg Ryan's famous faked-orgasm scene in the movie *When Harry Met Sally.* During the filming, Billy Crystal, a great Katz's fan, wolfed down six pastrami sandwiches! Try one (believe me, it's ample) with a potato knish and a cream soda. There's cafeteria and waiter service. Open Sunday to Tuesday from 8am to 9pm, Wednesdays and Thursdays from 8am to 10pm, Fridays and Saturdays from 8am to 11pm.

Our last stop is:

16. Russ and Daughters, 179 East Houston Street (tel. 475-4880). Joel and Bella Russ began selling food from a pushcart in 1911. Their operation evolved into one of New York's most famous appetizer stores, today run by their grandson Mark Federman. At this final stop on our tour, you can stock up on nova, creamed herring, whitefish salad, and other Jewish delicacies, and take a little of the Lower East Side home with you.

SoHo:
The Cast-Iron District

Start: West Broadway and Houston Street.
Subway: Take the C or E to Spring Street. Head north on Sullivan Street, make a right on Houston Street, and walk two blocks to the starting point.
Finish: Wooster Street between Prince and Spring Streets.
Time: Approximately 2 to 3 hours, depending on the length of time you spend browsing in shops and galleries.
Best Times: When the galleries are open, generally Tuesday through Saturday between about 10am to 6pm.
Worst Times: Sundays and Mondays.

Until the late 1840s, what we now call SoHo (a fractured acronym for *S*outh of *Ho*uston Street) was a quiet residential quarter on the northern edge of town. Starting in about 1850, a building boom (petering out finally in the 1890s) totally transformed the place into a neighborhood of pricey retail stores and loft buildings for light manufacturing. All this activity coincided with the development of cast iron as a building material. Columns, arches, pediments, brackets, keystones, and everything else that once had to be carved in stone could now be mass produced at lower cost in iron. The result was a commercial building spree that gave free rein to the opulent architectural style of the day.

But after the spree came long generations of neglect. By the late

1960s, the area was dismissed as too dismal for words. And for that precise reason, it began attracting impoverished artists. Back then you could rent huge spaces in SoHo's former sweatshops (considerable exploitation once went on behind these handsome facades) for next to nothing. But restless fashion was not about to ignore a developing new brew of art and historic architecture. By the early 1970s, the land boom was on. Today, West Broadway is literally lined with rarefied boutiques, avant-garde galleries, and trendy restaurants. SoHo lofts now appear in the pages of *Architectural Digest,* and they're more likely to be inhabited by art patrons than artists.

Yet one cannot dismiss SoHo as a travesty of art sold out to commerce. Its concentration of galleries soon made it a major force in world art markets, and as such, a major force in shaping today's art. The intellectual and artistic ferment in SoHo had strong parallels to what was happening in Paris and Berlin between the wars or in Greenwich Village at the turn of the century. The rediscovery of the old buildings is somewhat ironic (no pun intended) as they are about as spiritually distant from modern art as it is possible for buildings to be.

Take time to browse through the numerous shops and galleries along the tour route. Galleries here feature everything from the highly representational to concepts and constructions that challenge your entire definition of art. And the wares in SoHo shops are marvelously innovative and delightful. Note: Many buildings house numerous galleries on upper floors.

REFRESHMENT STOP   If you want to get an early start, plan breakfast at the **Elephant and Castle,** 183 Prince Street at Sullivan Street (tel. 260-3600). Options at this cozy neighborhood eatery range from eggs rancheros to French toast with real Vermont maple syrup and fresh fruit. It opens at 8:30am weekdays, 9am Saturdays, 10am Sundays.

Start at the corner of:

1. **West Broadway and Houston Street.** Walk south toward the World Trade Center towers that loom so picturesquely in the distance. Although this street is the center of the downtown gallery world, SoHo's most famous thoroughfare does not by a long shot contain the best cast-iron buildings. What makes West Broadway so famous—besides its numerous chic boutiques—is its concentration of noted art galleries. Although art as big business has faltered a bit of late, West Broadway's streetside atmosphere remains exciting and cosmopolitan.

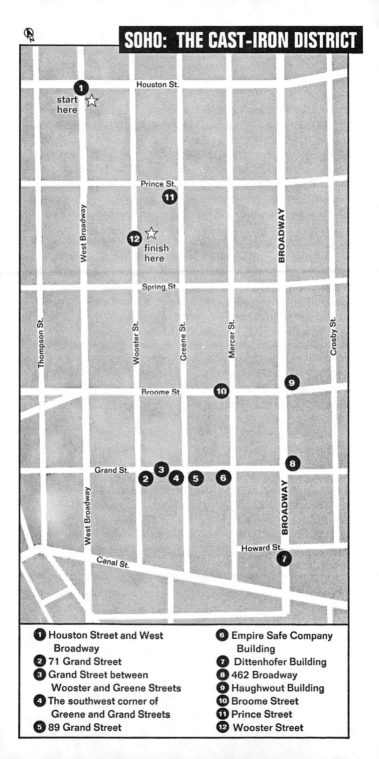

SOHO: THE CAST-IRON DISTRICT

Houston St.

① start here

Prince St.

⑪

⑫ finish here

Spring St.

West Broadway

Thompson St.

Wooster St.

Greene St.

Mercer St.

BROADWAY

Crosby St.

⑨

Broome St. ⑩

Grand St. ② ③ ④ ⑤ ⑥

⑧

West Broadway

BROADWAY

Howard St.

Canal St. ⑦

① Houston Street and West Broadway
② 71 Grand Street
③ Grand Street between Wooster and Greene Streets
④ The southwest corner of Greene and Grand Streets
⑤ 89 Grand Street
⑥ Empire Safe Company Building
⑦ Dittenhofer Building
⑧ 462 Broadway
⑨ Haughwout Building
⑩ Broome Street
⑪ Prince Street
⑫ Wooster Street

Turn left on Grand Street and head east to the intersection of Grand and Wooster Streets. Now we're really getting into cast-iron country. Note the renovated southeast corner building at:

2. **71 Grand Street.** Its marvelous Victorian facade (added in 1888), fronted by fluted Corinthian columns, is typical of what's been rediscovered down here. Structurally speaking, cast-iron buildings were not particularly innovative. They were usually supported by the same brick walls and timber floors as the buildings they replaced. The cast iron was merely mounted on the facade as a substitute for carved stone. Nor did it necessarily cover an entire facade. But it did have a definite look, as you'll see on the next block of:

3. **Grand Street between Wooster and Greene Streets.** Iron pillars seem to line the street into infinity. A century ago these sidewalks were crowded with shoppers. The ground floors of the buildings contained all manner of dry-goods emporiums, while the upper levels were jammed with immigrants crouched over sewing machines for 12 hours a day.

Continue on to the intersection of:

4. **Grand and Greene Streets.** On the southwest corner, you'll see a large off-white building (with the date 1872 noted under its cornice) that sums up the commercial aesthetic of those times. It is a real iron palace, lifted direct from the Italian Renaissance as interpreted by a 19th-century architect.

The cast-iron building at the southeast corner of the same intersection is:

5. **89 Grand Street,** and it sums up the SoHo of today: innovative, visually arresting, and expensive looking. Before we move on, glance up Greene Street for more cast-iron vistas. *Historical footnote:* During the cast-iron heyday of SoHo, Greene Street was one of New York's premier red-light districts.

Continue another block to the corner of Grand and Mercer Streets. Here the five-story:

6. **Empire Safe Company Building,** on the southwest side of the street, shows how cast iron was combined with other building materials. In this case, it's been confined to the first-floor facade, which doesn't look as if it's changed one bit in the last century.

Make a right on Mercer Street and a left on Howard Street (note ahead on Canal Street, Pearl Paint—supply central for New York artists) walking one block to the corner of Broadway. Here, you'll see the extravagant:

7. **Dittenhofer Building,** 429 Broadway, built in 1870 and faced with ornately embellished Corinthian cast-iron columns and arched windows.

Turn left on Broadway and walk uptown—on a block lined with fabric stores—to the corner of Grand Street. The beautiful cast-iron commercial building at:

8. **462 Broadway,** evoking French Renaissance architecture, shows the heavy hand of modernization on the first floor. Who could have really thought the modernish mess they've made of the street level was better than what was there in the first place?

REFRESHMENT STOP Having now trashed the renovated exterior architecture of 462 Broadway, I'll recommend the delightful restaurant occupying its space. Called **L'Ecole Bar/Restaurant** (tel. 219-3300), it's run by students of the French Culinary Institute. Fancy French fare (items like cassoulet of white beans with pork and goose or roast leg of lamb with spinach flan and almond potatoes) is served. Prices are moderate to high. Open for lunch Monday to Friday from noon to 2pm, dinner nightly from 6 to 9:30pm. Reservations suggested.

Continue north on Broadway to the Corinthian-pillared:

9. **Haughwout Building,** at 488–492 Broadway. Among other things, this 1857 Italianate building is noted for its original Otis elevator, still in service. The street-level showrooms—today housing an outlet store for bed and bath products—once glittered with the silver, chandeliers, and crystal goods sold by Eder Haughwout. While the original cream-colored paint job is a distant memory, the structure remains essentially unaltered, an evocative reminder of Broadway's former commercial glory.

Cross the street, and turn left into:

10. **Broome Street,** continuing two blocks to the intersection of Broome and Greene Streets. Much of SoHo, as you can see, remains pretty gritty and industrial, notwithstanding its historic buildings and trendy art culture. And yet a critical mass has definitely been achieved. Today, the dirtiest SoHo street corner manages somehow to look "fashionable," at least in the eyes of a downtown New Yorker.

Turn right into Greene Street and proceed two blocks to the corner of:

11. **Prince Street.** Before you reach Prince Street, you'll see examples of just about everything that's happening in SoHo these days. There are cast-iron buildings—some gloriously renovated, some still grotty—another clutch of galleries, a gorgeous condominium (in a renovated cast-iron building at 95–97 Greene Street that's clearly not being marketed to starving artists), plus various unglamorous tool and rag busi-

nesses. Pause for a moment at Prince and Greene, and look up at the eastern wall of 114 Prince Street, also called the SoHo Center. This cleverly painted trompe l'oeil wall re-creates the cast-iron street facade, complete to the painted cat in the painted open window.

REFRESHMENT STOPS **Dean & Deluca,** 121 Prince Street, between Greene and Wooster Streets (tel. 254-8776), offers exquisite gourmet salads (such as fettuccine with Thai shrimp), sandwiches, and desserts. Open Monday to Saturday from 8am to 8pm, on Sundays from 9am to 7pm.

I also like the **Prince Street Bar & Restaurant,** 125 Prince Street, at Wooster Street (tel. 228-8130), an archetypical SoHo eatery. Moderately priced menu offerings run the gamut from barbecued baby back ribs to tortellini alfredo to Indonesian specialties such as gado gado salad. Open Sunday to Tuesday from 11:30am to 11:30pm, Wednesday to Saturday 11:30am to midnight.

Go left on Prince Street, then left on Wooster Street.

12. Wooster Street, between Prince and Spring Streets, gives you one final block of shopping and gallery hopping.

WALKING TOUR 6

Greenwich Village
Literary Tour
Part I

Start: St. Luke's Place and Hudson Street.
Subway: Take the 1 or 9 to Houston Street. Walk west on Houston Street and make a right on Hudson Street to St. Luke's Place.
Finish: The White Horse Tavern, at Hudson and 11th Streets.
Time: Approximately 3 hours.
Best Times: Any time the weather is conducive to walking.

In the 19th century, when the Village was still considered a suburban retreat, it was New York's literary hub—a venue for salons and other gatherings of the intelligentsia. The 20th century saw the Village transformed from a bastion of aristocratic New York families to a bohemian enclave of writers, artists, and radicals. Though skyrocketing rents made the Village less accessible to impecunious artists after the late 1920s, it has remained a mecca for creative people. Though the focus of this tour—and the following one—is the area's literary history, you'll also enjoy strolling the winding Village streets, lined with elegant Federal and Greek Revival buildings. I promise, you'll get a good feel for one of the city's most fascinating neighborhoods.

Our tour starts at:

1. **6 St. Luke's Place.** St. Luke's Place is a charming old Village street lined with stately gingko trees and elegant mid-19th-century Italianate houses, several of which have been occupied by well-known writers. This brick town house, however, is not a literary landmark. It was the residence of the flamboyant Jimmy Walker when he was mayor of New York. He was notorious for frequenting speakeasies even during the height of Prohibition, and for enjoying an extravagant lifestyle while the Tammany Hall bosses tightened their grip on the city. After scandal forced him to resign as mayor, he left for Europe with his wife (a former show girl). The park across the street is named for him.

As you continue, you'll pass no. 10, which you may recognize from exterior shots of the Huxtable home in *The Cosby Show.* Our next stop is:

2. **12 St. Luke's Place.** Sherwood Anderson, hailed as the authentic voice of the Midwest after the publication of his novel *Winesburg, Ohio,* lived here in 1923.

Also on this block is:

3. **14 St. Luke's Place,** where poet Marianne Moore shared a ground-floor apartment with her mother from 1918 to 1929. Their rent was $25 a month.

Continue to:

4. **16 St. Luke's Place.** Theodore Dreiser lived on the parlor floor of this classic New York brownstone from 1922 to 1923; while he lived here he began writing *An American Tragedy.* Dreiser once told H. L. Mencken he had planned his last words. They were, "Shakespeare, I come!" I don't know if he managed to utter them.

Across the street is:

5. **The Hudson Park Library,** which has served the Village community since 1906. Poet Marianne Moore worked here as an assistant librarian from 1921 to 1925, earning $50 a month.

REFRESHMENT STOP Cent' Anni, 50 Carmine Street, between Bedford and Bleecker Streets (tel. 989-9494), rates three stars from *The New York Times* restaurant critic Mimi Sheraton. Ask for the fixed-price menu at lunch, and be sure to order the scrumptious zuppa ortolana—a baked soup rich with beans, cabbage, leeks, cheese, and toast, topped with fresh-grated parmesan. Open for lunch Monday through Friday from noon to 3pm, for dinner nightly from 5 to 11pm.

From St. Luke's Place, make a left on Seventh Avenue South and head uptown. Then turn left on Commerce Street to reach:

6. 11 Commerce Street. Washington Irving wrote *The Legend of Sleepy Hollow* while living in this quaint three-story brick building.

Continue walking west on Commerce and turn left at Bedford Street to find:

7. 75½ Bedford Street. The narrowest house in the Village (a mere 9½ feet across), this unlikely three-story brick residence was built on the site of a former carriage alley in 1873. Edna St. Vincent Millay lived here from 1923 (the year she won a Pulitzer Prize for her poetry) to 1925. Other famous residents were Cary Grant and John Barrymore. The house has seen better days; today it's uninhabited, the windows are boarded up, and the house number is merely scribbled on the door in magic marker.

Return to Commerce Street, where:

8. The Cherry Lane Theatre, nestled in a bend at 38 Commerce Street, was founded in 1924 by Edna St. Vincent Millay. Famed scenic designer Cleon Throckmorton transformed the Revolutionary-era building (originally a silo on a farm here, later a factory) into a playhouse that became prominent presenting works by Edward Albee, Samuel Beckett, Eugene Ionesco, Jean Genet, and Harold Pinter. In 1951, Judith Malina and Julian Beck founded the ultraexperimental Living Theatre on its premises. And before rising to megafame, Barbra Streisand worked as a Cherry Lane usher.

At the end of Commerce Street, make a left into Barrow Street and a right on Hudson Street. On Hudson and Grove Streets is:

9. St. Luke in the Fields, one of the oldest churches in Manhattan, built in 1822. The original chapel was gutted by fire in 1981, but neighborhood residents rallied and came to the rescue with contributions to finance its rebuilding. The church reopened in 1985. One of its founding vestrymen, Clement Moore, wrote *'Twas the Night Before Christmas,* published in 1823 as *A Visit from St. Nicholas.* St. Luke was also the venue for Dylan Thomas's funeral in 1953.

Next door is:

10. 487 Hudson Street. This 1827 house, presently the Parish House of St. Luke, was the boyhood home of Bret Harte, author of *The Luck of Roaring Camp* and *Stories of the Sierras.*

Now turn right into Grove Street and make another right on Bedford Street to:

11. Chumley's, 86 Bedford Street (tel. 675-4449), which opened in 1926 and operated clandestinely as a speakeasy during Prohibition, with a casino hidden away upstairs. Its convoluted entranceway with four steps up and four down (designed to slow police raiders), the lack of a sign outside, and a back door that opens on to an alleyway to Barrow Street are remnants of this era.

Chumley's has always been a writer's bar. Its walls are lined with book jackets of works by famous patrons who, over the years, have included Edna St. Vincent Millay (she once lived upstairs), John Steinbeck, Eugene O'Neill, e.e. cummings, Edna Ferber, John Dos Passos, Theodore Dreiser, William Faulkner, Gregory Corso, Norman Mailer, William Carlos Williams, Allen Ginsberg, Lionel Trilling, Nicholas Pileggi, Harvey Fierstein, Calvin Trillin, and numerous others. Even the elusive J. D. Salinger hoisted a few at the bar here, and Simone de Beauvoir came by when she was in town.

With its working fireplaces, wood-plank flooring, old carved-up oak tables, and amber lighting, Chumley's lacks nothing in the way of mellowed atmosphere. Think about returning for drinks or dinner. A blackboard menu features fresh pasta and grilled fish. Open nightly from 5pm to an arbitrary closing time, Chumley's also offers brunch on weekends from 11am to 4pm.

Double back to Grove Street, which was named in the 19th century for its many gardens and groves, to look for:

12. 17 Grove Street. Parts of this wood-frame house date to the early 1800s. The top floor was added in 1870 (the exterior colors—tan and rust—reflect this era), and the present owners created a downstairs level in 1989. A friend of James Baldwin lived here in the 1960s, and Baldwin frequently stayed at the house.

Further along is:

13. 45 Grove Street. Poet Hart Crane lived in this late Federal–period residence (built in 1830, refurbished with Italianate influences in 1870). Originally a freestanding two-story building, it was, in the 19th century, one of the Village's most elegant mansions, surrounded by verdant lawns with greenhouses and stables on the premises. In the movie *Reds,* 45 Grove was portrayed as Eugene O'Neill's house (Jack Nicholson played O'Neill). Crane began writing his poetic portrait of America, *The Bridge,* here in the late 1920s. In 1932, at the age of 33, he committed suicide by jumping from a ship into the Gulf of Mexico.

Continue on Grove Street, make a right at Bleecker Street, and look for:

14. 309 Bleecker Street. Thomas Paine lived in a small two-story wooden house at this location, today a Gristede's super-market.

Head east on Bleecker Street, turn left on Seventh Avenue, and walk uptown for a block. To your left is:

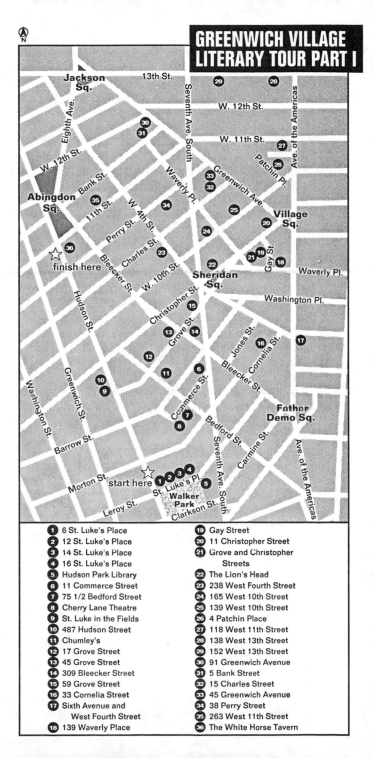

GREENWICH VILLAGE
LITERARY TOUR PART I

1 6 St. Luke's Place
2 12 St. Luke's Place
3 14 St. Luke's Place
4 16 St. Luke's Place
5 Hudson Park Library
6 11 Commerce Street
7 75 1/2 Bedford Street
8 Cherry Lane Theatre
9 St. Luke in the Fields
10 487 Hudson Street
11 Chumley's
12 17 Grove Street
13 45 Grove Street
14 309 Bleecker Street
15 59 Grove Street
16 33 Cornelia Street
17 Sixth Avenue and
       West Fourth Street
18 139 Waverly Place

19 Gay Street
20 11 Christopher Street
21 Grove and Christopher
       Streets
22 The Lion's Head
23 238 West Fourth Street
24 165 West 10th Street
25 139 West 10th Street
26 4 Patchin Place
27 118 West 11th Street
28 138 West 13th Street
29 152 West 13th Street
30 91 Greenwich Avenue
31 5 Bank Street
32 15 Charles Street
33 45 Greenwich Avenue
34 38 Perry Street
35 263 West 11th Street
36 The White Horse Tavern

15. **59 Grove Street.** Political theorist and writer Thomas Paine—whose tract, *The Crisis,* begins with the words "These are the times that try men's souls"—died here in 1809. The downstairs space has always been a restaurant, today Marie's Crisis Café (tel. 243-9323). Though the building Paine lived in burned down, some of the interior brickwork is original. Of note, behind the bar, is a WPA-era mural (done with metals on mirror) depicting the French and American Revolutions and bearing the mottoes *"Liberté, Egalité, Fraternité"* and "Rights of Man." Up a flight of stairs is another mural (this a wood-relief carving) called *La Convention.* It depicts Robespierre, Danton, and Thomas Paine, and is inscribed with Danton's inspirational words of 1792, *"De l'audace, et encore de l'audace, et toujours de l'audace!"* In the 1920s, you might have spotted anyone from Eugene O'Neill to Edward VIII of England here. Today, Marie's is a lively piano bar (everyone sings along) that's open nightly from 9:30pm to 3:30am.

    Head back to Seventh Avenue and double back downtown again. Turn left on Bleecker Street, then left again on Cornelia, and look for:

16. **33 Cornelia Street.** Throughout the 1940s, James Agee lived on Bleecker Street and worked in a studio at this address. The building is fronted by an early 1800s blacksmith shop.

    Nearby, at 31 Cornelia Street, once stood the long-vanished **Caffè Cino,** which opened as a coffeehouse in 1958. In the early 1960s, the owner began to encourage aspiring playwrights—such as Lanford Wilson, Sam Shepard, and John Guare—to stage readings and performances here. Their experimentation in this tiny café space gave birth to New York's off-off-Broadway theater.

    At the end of Cornelia Street, you'll come to the junction of:

17. **Sixth Avenue and West 4th Street.** Eugene O'Neill frequented a bar called the Golden Swan (better known as the "Hell Hole") at this corner and later used it as a setting for his play *The Iceman Cometh.* A recycling center occupies the bar's former site.

    Head north on Sixth Avenue for a couple of blocks and make a left on Waverly Place to reach:

18. **139 Waverly Place.** Edna St. Vincent Millay lived here with her sister Norma in 1918. An interesting note: Edna St. Vincent Millay's middle name was derived from St. Vincent's Hospital, which had saved her uncle's life.

    Continue walking west and make a right at:

19. **Gay Street.** Famous residents of this tiny street (originally a stable alley) have included New York Mayor Jimmy Walker, who owned the 18th-century town house at no. 12. A more recent

owner of this building was Frank Paris, creator of *Howdy Doody*. Ruth McKenney lived in the basement of no. 14 with her sister Eileen, who later married Nathanael West. It was the setting for McKenney's popular stage comedy, *My Sister Eileen*. The house dates to 1827. Mary McCarthy, the *Partisan Review*'s drama critic and author, lived at no. 18.

On the other side of Gay Street is:

20. **11 Christopher Street.** In 1918, e.e. cummings and William Slater Brown shared an apartment at this address, today a parking lot. Cummings and Brown (a pal from Harvard days) had both been imprisoned for several months while stationed in France as ambulance drivers during World War I. The charge: writing letters that military censors regarded (erroneously) as treasonous. Basically, the two young men (Brown was 21, cummings 23), seemed to view the whole experience as a lark. Cummings wrote home to his parents, "Our life here is A 1. Never have I so appreciated leisure. I continually write notes on painting, poetry, and sculpture, as well as music, and the Muse Herself has not been unkind." Another letter describes "days spent with an inimitable friend [Brown] in soul-stretching probings of aesthetics . . . and fine folk to converse in five or six languages . . . perfection attained at last." Cummings wrote about their imprisonment in *The Enormous Room*.

Walking west along Christopher Street, which is the heart of New York's gay community, you'll pass the Oscar Wilde Memorial Bookshop, which specializes in gay publications, en route to:

21. **Grove and Christopher Streets.** The wedge-shaped Georgian Northern Dispensary Building on the corner dates to 1831. Edgar Allan Poe was treated for a head cold here in 1836.

Further west is:

22. **The Lion's Head,** 59 Christopher Street (tel. 929-0670), has been a writer's bar/media hangout since its inception in 1958 (it's occupied this location since 1966). Jessica Lange worked here as a waitress before rising to Hollywood fame. A Lion's Head bartender once described the bar as a place for "writers with a drinking problem," which a customer later amended to a place for "drinkers with a writing problem." Another bartender characterized the clientele as "Irishmen who write like Jews and Jews who drink like Irishmen." When Norman Mailer ran for mayor in the 1960s, Joe Flaherty ran his campaign from the bar. Jack Newfield and Pete Hamill talked Bobby Kennedy into running for president at the round table in the back. Other Lion's Head regulars have included Dennis Hamill, Jimmy Breslin, and scores of TV newspeople such as Tony Guida and Linda Ellerbee. The walls are lined with book jackets from the

works of the regular customers. Open daily except Christmas from noon to 4am.

Make a right on West 4th Street and look for:

23. 238 West 4th Street. Edward Albee wrote *The Zoo Story* in three weeks at the kitchen table of his apartment here. The play was presented at the Provincetown Playhouse in 1960.

Turn around and walk back to 10th Street. Make a left to find:

24. 165 West 10th Street. Theodore Dreiser lived here from 1914 to 1920, during which time he wrote *The "Genius,"* an autobiographically inspired novel, published in 1915 and immediately declared obscene and banned by the Society for the Suppression of Vice. After many court battles, Dreiser—who was championed by H. L. Mencken—managed to get *The "Genius"* back into bookstores in 1923. It was not the first—or the last—time Dreiser tangled with censors. *Sister Carrie,* his first novel, was suppressed because its heroine, "a fallen woman," triumphantly escapes the "wages of sin." And *An American Tragedy* also inspired the wrath of the Mrs. Grundys. During Dreiser's tenancy, Edgar Lee Masters read his *Spoon River* poems at a party here. The building Dreiser lived in was demolished and replaced by a newer structure.

Continue in the same direction, crossing Waverly Place, to:

25. 139 West 10th Street. The Ninth Circle has been a popular Village watering hole for decades, but it was at a bar that used to occupy this site that playwright Edward Albee saw graffiti scrawled on a mirror reading, "Who's afraid of Virginia Woolf?" and appropriated it.

REFRESHMENT STOP **The Peacock Caffè,** 24 Greenwich Avenue, between West 10th and Charles Streets (tel. 242-9395), a Village institution since 1946, has always been a popular spot. Originally an art gallery-cum-coffee shop, the Peacock retains much of its early bohemian ambience in the way of rococo columns, walls hung with 17th-century Italian oil paintings, and recordings of operatic arias that provide a mellow musical backdrop. The menu features salads, pastas, sandwiches, and Italian pastries. Open Sunday to Thursday from 1pm to 1am, on Fridays and Saturdays till 2am, on Mondays till midnight.

From West 10th Street, cross Greenwich Avenue and walk a block to:

26. Patchin Place. This tranquil, tree-shaded cul-de-sac has sheltered many illustrious residents: e.e. cummings lived at no. 4 from 1923 to 1962, where his visitors included T. S. Eliot, Ezra Pound, and Dylan Thomas. The highly acclaimed but not widely known Djuna Barnes (whom literary critics have compared to James Joyce) lived in a tiny one-room apartment at no. 5. Reclusive and eccentric, she almost never left the premises over a 40-year period, prompting cummings to occasionally shout from his window, "Are you still alive, Djuna?" Barnes wrote a memoir called *Life Is Painful, Nasty, & Short . . . In My Case It Has Only Been Nasty* (she lived to the age of 90). Though he was usually elsewhere, John Reed maintained a residence at Patchin Place from 1895 until his death in 1920 and wrote *Ten Days That Shook the World* there. Theodore Dreiser and English poet laureate John Masefield are additional past Patchin Place residents. The gate opens; you can go inside.

Walk east to Sixth Avenue and make a left, then make another left at 11th Street to:

27. 118 West 11th Street. Theodore Dreiser completed *An American Tragedy* in a no-longer-extant town house here that is today part of P. S. 41.

Walk back to Sixth Avenue and head north, making a left on 13th Street to:

28. 138 West 13th Street. Max Eastman and other radicals fomented revolution in the pages of *The Liberator*, headquartered in this lovely building on a pleasant tree-lined street. The magazine published works by John Reed, as well as Edna St. Vincent Millay, Ernest Hemingway, Elinor Wylie, e.e. cummings (who later became very right-wing and a passionate supporter of Senator Joseph McCarthy's Communist witch-hunts), John Dos Passos, and William Carlos Williams. *The Liberator* succeeded *The Masses*, an earlier Eastman publication (see Stop 30).

Further west along the block is:

29. 152 West 13th Street. Offices of the *Dial*, a major literary magazine of the 1920s, occupied this beautiful Greek Revival brick town house. The magazine dated back to 1840, with Ralph Waldo Emerson as editor. T. S. Eliot first published *The Waste Land* in the *Dial*, and Marianne Moore edited the magazine from 1925 to its final issue in 1929.

Continue west on 13th Street and make a left on Seventh Avenue, a right on 12th Street, and then another left to:

30. 91 Greenwich Avenue. At the beginning of the 20th century, Max Eastman was editor of a radical left-wing literary magazine called *The Masses*, which published, among others, John Reed, Carl Sandburg, Sherwood Anderson, Upton Sinclair, Edgar Lee Masters, e.e. cummings, and Louis Untermeyer. The magazine was suppressed by the Justice Department in 1918 because of its opposition to World War I, and several of its staff were put on trial under the Espionage Act and charged with conspiracy to obstruct recruiting and prevent enlistment. Pacifist Edna St. Vincent Millay read poems to the accused to help pass the time while juries were out. Offices of *The Masses* were at this address, today a video-rental store. So much for today's cultural scene.

Head east on Greenwich Avenue, make a right on Bank Street, and look for:

31. 5 Bank Street. In 1913, Willa Cather moved to a seven-room, second-floor apartment in a large brick house at this address, where she wrote *My Antonia, Death Comes to the Archbishop,* and several other novels (they're listed on a plaque out front). When she became successful, she rented the apartment above hers and kept it empty to ensure perfect quiet. Her Friday afternoon at-homes here were frequented by D. H. Lawrence, among others.

REFRESHMENT STOP   Ye Waverly Inn, 16 Bank Street, at Waverly Place (tel. 929-4377), nestles cozily on the lower floor of an 1844 inn. It consists of a warren of rooms with low-beamed ceilings, blazing hearths, and lace-curtained windows. The old carriage courtyard today provides outdoor seating. The food is traditional American fare, such as chicken pot pie and roast turkey with cornbread stuffing. Robert de Niro often filled up with fried chicken here when he was trying to gain weight for *Raging Bull.* And in days of yore, Edna St. Vincent Millay was a frequent customer. Open for dinner Monday to Thursday from 5:15 to 10pm, Fridays and Saturdays from 5:15 to 11pm, and Sundays from 4:30 to 9pm; brunch is served on Saturdays and Sundays from 11:30am to 3pm.

From Bank Street, start heading down Waverly Place and then turn left on Charles Street to find:

32. 15 Charles Street. Richard Wright owned a mid-19th-century brownstone here from 1945 to 1947, now sadly replaced by a modern apartment building with all the charm of a prison.

Turn left on Greenwich Avenue to:

33. 45 Greenwich Avenue. William Styron moved here in 1951, after the success of his first novel, *Lie Down in Darkness.*

Head west on Greenwich Avenue and make a left on Perry Street to reach:

34. 38 Perry Street. When James Agee graduated from Harvard in 1932, he moved into a basement apartment here, which he occupied for five years. The building, which dates to 1845, had a backyard garden and porch.

Continue west on Perry Street, make a right on West 4th Street, and then a left on West 11th Street to:

35. 263 West 11th Street. After he became successful, Thomas Wolfe and his lover, set designer Aline Bernstein, moved to these elegant digs. Wolfe rhapsodized over this home (though he placed it on 12th Street) in the opening pages of his novel *You Can't Go Home Again*: ". . . its red brick walls, its rooms of noble height and spaciousness, its old dark woods and floors that creaked; and in the magic of the moment it seemed to be enriched and given a profound and lonely dignity by all the human beings it had sheltered in its ninety years. . . ." The building dates to the 19th century, and its front door and facade are the same as when Wolfe lived here. The brick has recently been cleaned.

Continue west on 11th Street to:

36. The White Horse Tavern, 567 Hudson Street (tel. 989-3956), which dates back to 1880. I especially love the front room, with its original 19th-century mahogany bar, oak backbar, and pressed-tin ceiling. Over the decades, it has served everyone from Thomas Wolfe to Joan Didion. The White Horse was a famous literary hangout of the 1950s, when Dan Wolf, founder of the *Village Voice,* and Norman Mailer initiated Sunday-afternoon gatherings here. Jack Kerouac, Pete Hamill, Jimmy Breslin, Joe Flaherty, Allen Ginsberg, and James Baldwin were among the attendees. Mailer liked it because, he said, "if you invited people to your house, it was not that easy to get rid of them." The tavern's most famous tippler was Welsh poet Dylan Thomas, who collapsed a few steps from the door one night (legend has it after gulping down 18 shots of whiskey in less than 20 minutes) and was taken to nearby St. Vincent's Hospital, where he died several days later. He was 39 years old. You can sit at his favorite table in the center room, which is marked by a plaque. Stop by for a pint of draft beer, hot buttered rum, or a meal (pub fare—burgers, salads, steaks, and sandwiches—is featured). The White Horse is open Sunday through Thursday from 11am to 2am, Fridays and Saturdays from 11am to 4am.

Greenwich Village Literary Tour Part II

Start: Bleecker Street between La Guardia Place and Thompson Street.
Subway: Take the 6 to Bleecker Street, which lets you out at Bleecker and Lafayette Streets. Walk west on Bleecker.
Finish: 14 West 10th Street.
Time: Approximately 2½ hours.
Best Times: Any time the weather is conducive to walking.

Like the preceding tour, the walk below concentrates on the people and places that figure prominently in the literary history of the Village. This tour covers an area just east of the route we followed in the other walk; it centers around Washington Square Park, the hub of the Village, where you can follow in the footsteps of Henry James and Edith Wharton.

Begin at:

1. **145 Bleecker Street,** where James Fenimore Cooper, author of *The Last of the Mohicans,* lived in 1833. His friend Samuel F. B. Morse (of Morse code fame) found the house for him.
   Continue west to:
2. **160 Bleecker Street.** This palatial beaux arts–style lodging, designed as the Mills Hotel (for men of modest means) by noted

architect Ernest Flagg, was the first New York address of Theodore Dreiser in 1895. His rent was 25¢ a night.

Across the street, the:

3. **Circle in the Square Theatre,** at 159 Bleecker Street, was founded in 1951 at the site of an abandoned nightclub on Sheridan Square. It moved to Bleecker Street in 1959. One of the first arena theaters in the United States, it rose to prominence producing works by Eugene O'Neill and Tennessee Williams. Williams's *Summer and Smoke* (starring Geraldine Page), Thorton Wilder's *Plays for Bleecker Street,* and Jean Genet's *The Balcony* premiered here, and actors Colleen Dewhurst, Dustin Hoffman, James Earl Jones, Cicely Tyson, Jason Robards, George C. Scott, and Peter Falk honed their craft on the Circle in the Square stage. Since 1972, the theater has had an additional stage uptown at 50th Street and Broadway. At both locations, it presents high-quality productions of important plays.

Further west is:

4. **172 Bleecker Street.** After he completed *Let Us Now Praise Famous Men,* writer James Agee lived in a railroad flat here from 1941 to 1951.

Nearby is the:

5. **Café Figaro,** at 184–186 Bleecker Street, which was a beat-generation haunt. In 1969 Village residents were disheartened to see the Figaro close and in its place arise a sterile-looking Blimpie's. Miraculously, in 1976, the present owner completely restored the Figaro to its earlier appearance, replastering its walls with shellacked copies of the French newspaper *Le Figaro.* Having personally whiled away many leisurely hours here over cappuccino and intense conversation in the 1960s, I can vouch for the total authenticity of the restoration.

Further along the street, past MacDougal Street, is:

6. **190 Bleecker Street,** the birthplace of beat poet Gregory Corso in 1930. How hip can you get? Bleecker Street, by the way, was named for a writer, Anthony Bleecker, whose friends included Washington Irving and William Cullen Bryant. The Bleecker family farm occupied this area.

Across the way is:

7. **189 Bleecker Street.** For several decades, beginning in the late 1940s, **The San Remo** (today **Carpo's Café**), an Italian restaurant at the corner of Bleecker and MacDougal Streets, was a writers' hangout frequented by James Baldwin, William Styron, Jack Kerouac, James Agee, Frank O'Hara, Gregory Corso, Dylan Thomas, William Burroughs, and Allen Ginsberg.

Head north on MacDougal Street to the:

8. **Minetta Tavern,** 113 MacDougal Street, at Minetta Lane (tel.

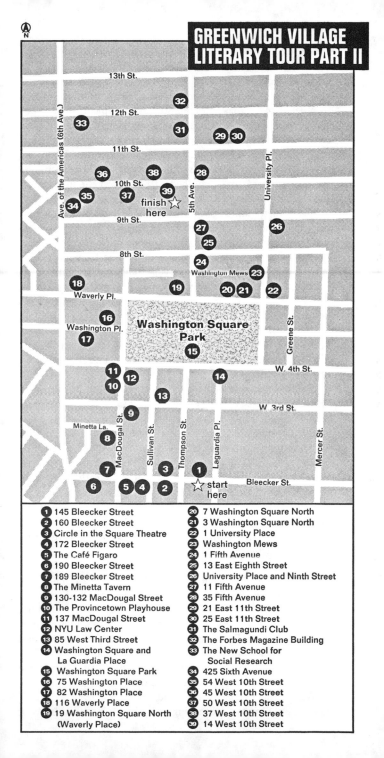

GREENWICH VILLAGE LITERARY TOUR PART II

N

Ave. of the Americas (6th Ave.)

13th St.
12th St.
11th St.
10th St.
9th St.
8th St.

Waverly Pl.

Washington Pl.

Washington Square Park

Minetta La.

MacDougal St.

Sullivan St.

Thompson St.

Laguardia Pl.

Mercer St.

University Pl.

5th Ave.

Greene St.

W. 4th St.

W. 3rd St.

Bleecker St.

finish here

start here

Washington Mews

1. 145 Bleecker Street
2. 160 Bleecker Street
3. Circle in the Square Theatre
4. 172 Bleecker Street
5. The Café Figaro
6. 190 Bleecker Street
7. 189 Bleecker Street
8. The Minetta Tavern
9. 130-132 MacDougal Street
10. The Provincetown Playhouse
11. 137 MacDougal Street
12. NYU Law Center
13. 85 West Third Street
14. Washington Square and La Guardia Place
15. Washington Square Park
16. 75 Washington Place
17. 82 Washington Place
18. 116 Waverly Place
19. 19 Washington Square North (Waverly Place)
20. 7 Washington Square North
21. 3 Washington Square North
22. 1 University Place
23. Washington Mews
24. 1 Fifth Avenue
25. 13 East Eighth Street
26. University Place and Ninth Street
27. 11 Fifth Avenue
28. 35 Fifth Avenue
29. 21 East 11th Street
30. 25 East 11th Street
31. The Salmagundi Club
32. The Forbes Magazine Building
33. The New School for Social Research
34. 425 Sixth Avenue
35. 54 West 10th Street
36. 45 West 10th Street
37. 50 West 10th Street
38. 37 West 10th Street
39. 14 West 10th Street

475-3850), which was a speakeasy called The Black Rabbit during Prohibition. Since 1937, it has been a cozily simpatico Italian restaurant and a meeting place for writers and other creative folk, including Ezra Pound, e.e. cummings, Louis Bromfield, and Ernest Hemingway. Archetypical Village bohemian Joe Gould—who spent 30 years gathering material for his lifework, a never-published book called *An Oral History of Our Time*—made it his headquarters. And the very unbohemian *Reader's Digest* was founded on the premises in 1923 and published in the basement in its early days.

The Minetta still evokes the old Village. Walls are covered with photographs and caricatures of famous patrons, and the rustic pine-paneled back room is adorned with murals of local landmarks. Stop in for a drink or a meal. The Minetta is open daily from noon to midnight, serving traditional Italian fare.

Minetta Lane, by the way, is named for the Minetta Brook that started on 23rd Street and flowed through here en route to the Hudson. The brook still runs underground.

Uptown and across the street stands:

9. **130–132 MacDougal Street.** Louisa May Alcott lived in this 1852 house, which is fronted by twin entrances and an ironwork portico.

On the other side of the street, just past West 3rd Street, is:

10. **The Provincetown Playhouse,** at 133 MacDougal Street (tel. 477-5048). Housed in a converted stable, the Playhouse was founded by Eugene O'Neill in 1917 and managed by him for a decade. Many of his early plays—*Bound East for Cardiff, The Hairy Ape,* and *The Emperor Jones,* among them—premiered here. Other seminal figures in the theater's early days were George Cram Cook, Susan Glaspell, Max Eastman, Edna St. Vincent Millay, Djuna Barnes, Edna Ferber, and John Reed. Katharine Cornell, Tallulah Bankhead, Bette Davis, and Eva Le Gallienne appeared on the Provincetown stage in its early years.

A little further uptown is:

11. **137 MacDougal Street.** Jack London, Upton Sinclair, Vachel Lindsay, Louis Untermeyer, Max Eastman, Theodore Dreiser, Lincoln Steffens, and Sinclair Lewis hashed over life theories at The Liberal Club, "A Meeting Place for Those Interested in New Ideas," on the second floor of a house at this address. Margaret Sanger lectured the club on birth control, and Sherwood Anderson read his plays. Downstairs were Polly's Restaurant (run by anarchists Polly Holliday and Hippolyte Havel) and the Washington Square Book Shop.

Across MacDougal Street stands the:

12. **NYU Law Center,** occupying a city block bounded by West

3rd, MacDougal, Sullivan, and West 4th Streets. It is on the site of a previous building, 42 Washington Square, where Lincoln Steffens lived. Another famed resident of no. 42—writer, war correspondent, and later Communist, John Reed (portrayed by Warren Beatty in the movie *Reds*)—wrote about the building in a lengthy, youthful paean titled *The Day in Bohemia or Life Among the Artists.* Dedicated to his friend Steffens, it includes the lines:

> *But nobody questions your morals,*
> *And nobody asks for the rent,*
> *There's no one to pry, if we're tight, you and I,*
> *Or demand how our evenings are spent.*
> *The furniture's ancient but plenty,*
> *The linen is spotless and fair,*
> *O life is a joy to a broth of a boy*
> *At Forty-two Washington Square!*

Steffens, like Reed, was a radical. After visiting post-Revolutionary Russia in 1919, he claimed, "I have seen the future, and it works." Eugene O'Neill also lived in this building during World War I, when he was having an affair with Louise Bryant, John Reed's lover (Diane Keaton in the movie). That affair, by the way, inspired O'Neill's 1927 drama, *Strange Interlude.*

The Law Center additionally encompasses 144 MacDougal Street, where, in 1942, Anaïs Nin rented a studio, installed a printing press, and published a novel (*Winter of Artifice*) and a collection of stories titled *Under a Glass Bell,* as well as a book of Max Ernst drawings.

Head back down the way you came on MacDougal Street and make a left on West 3rd Street to reach:

13. 85 West 3rd Street. Edgar Allan Poe lived on the third floor (his window is in the right-hand corner if you care to gaze) of this very unusual-looking building from 1844 to 1885. Today, it's part of NYU Law School, and the current residents claim his rooms are haunted.

Continue in the same direction to La Guardia Place and make a left to:

14. Washington Square and La Guardia Place. NYU's Loeb Student Center was once Madame Branchard's Rooming House, where tenants, at various times, included Stephen Crane, O. Henry, Willa Cather, John Dos Passos, Pierre Matisse, Upton Sinclair, and Theodore Dreiser. Because of its many illustrious occupants—described in the above-mentioned poem by John Reed as:

> *". . . Inglorious Miltons by the score—*
> *Mute Wagners—Rembrandts, ten or more—*
> *And Rodins . . . one to every floor . . ."*

—its seedy studios were known as the "genius houses."

Across the street is:

15. Washington Square Park. What is today Washington Square Park, the hub of the Village, began as a swamp frequented largely by duck hunters. Minetta Brook meandered through it. In the 18th and early 19th centuries, it was a potter's field (over 10,000 people are buried under the park) and an execution site. Some of the trees still standing were used as gallows.

The park was dedicated in 1826, and elegant residential dwellings—some of which have survived NYU's cannibalization of the neighborhood—went up around the square. The white marble Memorial Arch at the Fifth Avenue entrance—which in 1892 replaced a wooden arch erected in 1889 to commemorate the centenary of Washington's inauguration—was designed by Stanford White. One night in 1917, a group of pranksters—among them artists John Sloan and Marcel Duchamp and some actors from the Provincetown Playhouse—climbed the Washington Square Arch, fired cap guns, and proclaimed the "independent republic of Greenwich Village," a Utopia dedicated to "socialism, sex, poetry, conversation, dawn-greeting, anything—so long as it is taboo in the Middle West."

Walk through the park and exit on the west side to:

16. 75 Washington Place. A restaurant called Marta's at this site was a favorite in the 1920s of Elinor Wylie, John Dos Passos, and other writers. The building dates to the mid-1800s. In 1991, Marta's became an Italian restaurant called Stella (tel. 673-4025)—and it happens to be a great place to eat. Moderate fixed-price meals are available at lunch. Open Monday to Saturday from noon to 3pm for lunch, from 5 to 10:30pm for dinner.

Continue in the same direction. Across the street is:

17. 82 Washington Place. Willa Cather lived in this six-story apartment building. A later resident (in 1945) was Richard Wright. Band leader John Philip Sousa owned the 1839 building next door (no. 80).

Make a right on Sixth Avenue, then another right on Waverly Place to find:

18. 116 Waverly Place. In the 1840s, poet Anne Charlotte Lynch presided over salons here in a parlor with two blazing fireplaces. William Cullen Bryant, Horace Greeley, and Herman Melville were frequent guests, and Poe read his latest poem, *The Raven,* to the assembled literati. (Waverly Place, by the way, was named in 1833 for Sir Walter Scott's Novel, *Waverley*.) The current building on this site is of later vintage, dating to 1891.

Continue walking east. When you get to the northwest corner of the park, note the towering English elm; it was a hanging tree when the park was an execution ground. Opposite the park once stood:

19. **19 Washington Square North (Waverly Place).** Henry James's grandmother lived at this now-defunct address, and young Henry spent much time at her house—the inspiration for his novel *Washington Square*. Today, the site is occupied by an apartment building (2 Fifth Avenue). The no. 19 that exists today is a different house (the numbering system has changed since James's day).

Further east is:

20. **7 Washington Square North,** where Edith Wharton (*The Age of Innocence, House of Mirth, Ethan Frome*) and her mother lived in 1882. It was also once the home of Alexander Hamilton.

Nearby is:

21. **3 Washington Square North.** Critic Edmund Wilson moved to the Village after he graduated from Princeton and became managing editor of the *New Republic*. He lived in this house from 1921 to 1923. Another resident, John Dos Passos, wrote *Manhattan Transfer* here.

Make a left at University Place to find:

22. **1 University Place.** In the early 1920s, poet Elinor Wylie lived in this building, where she entertained Edmund Wilson, John Dos Passos, and others. She worked at *Vanity Fair* as its poetry editor. After Edmund Wilson married actress Mary Blair in 1923, they, too, moved to 1 University Place. The current building at this address dates to 1929.

Cross the street and turn left into:

23. **Washington Mews.** This picturesque 19th-century cobblestoned street, lined with vine-covered two-story buildings (converted stables and carriage houses constructed to serve posh Washington Square town houses), has had several famous residents, among them John Dos Passos, artist Edward Hopper (no. 14A), and Sherwood Anderson (no. 54). The latter building dates to 1834.

Continue to the end of Washington Mews, and then turn right to look for:

24. **1 Fifth Avenue.** Poet Sara Teasdale lived here from 1931 until 1933, when she committed suicide by overdosing on barbiturates. Jenny Jerome, Winston Churchill's mother, went to school in a building on this site. The current building dates to 1929.

Continue on Fifth Avenue, turning right at 8th Street to find:

25. 13 East 8th Street. Thomas Wolfe lived here with his mistress, stage designer Aline Bernstein, in a converted cold-water sweatshop loft. He began working on *Look Homeward Angel* here. Today, the building he lived in is replaced by a tacky food shop, but across the street, between University Place and Fifth Avenue, there are still many beautiful old buildings that will give you the flavor of the street in Wolfe's time.

Continue in the same direction, and make a left at University Place to the intersection of:

26. University Place and 9th Street. The café at the Lafayette Hotel on this southeast corner was a very popular gathering spot for writers, artists, and bohemians in the early 1920s. Today, it is the **Knickerbocker Bar & Grill** (tel. 228-8490), a comfortable wood-paneled restaurant and jazz club. Writers—Jack Newfield, E. L. Doctorow, Erica Jong, Sidney Zion, Christopher Cerf—still frequent the bar, which happens to be an historic one. Charles Lindbergh signed the contract for his transatlantic flight at this very bar. The Knickerbocker is open daily for lunch and dinner and offers live jazz Wednesday through Sunday from 9:45pm. The menu is American/continental.

Turn left on 9th Street, and make a left at Fifth Avenue. Just downtown is:

27. 11 Fifth Avenue. Today, the block-long Brevoort Apartments encompass several past literary addresses, including the old Brevoort Hotel that stood on the northeast corner of Fifth Avenue and 8th Street. The hotel's basement café was frequented by Isadora Duncan, Lincoln Steffens, John Reed, Emma Goldman, Walter Lippman, Theodore Dreiser, Eugene O'Neill, Edna St. Vincent Millay, and others. Both Nathanael West and James T. Farrell lived at the Brevoort from 1935 to 1936, the latter while writing *Studs Lonigan.*

Mark Twain lived in a majestic Neo-Gothic brownstone designed by noted architect James Renwick, Jr., now sadly demolished and also part of the Brevoort Apartments. (Renwick also created magnificent St. Patrick's Cathedral and Grace Church.) There Twain wrote and received visitors while prone in a gigantic Italianate bed. Washington Irving was an earlier resident.

And Mable Dodge, a lover of John Reed, hosted a popular salon in a decaying mansion at 23 Fifth Avenue (on the corner of 9th Street) in 1913. Each week the meeting had a different theme for discussion—psychoanalysis, birth control, free love, the unemployed, and so on. The air was always "vibrant with intellectual excitement and electrical with the appearance of new ideas and dawning changes." Marsden Hartley and John

Marin talked about theories of modern art, Emma Goldman preached anarchy, and John Reed organized everyone in aid of striking workers. The guest list comprised all of the basement café crowd described above.

Turn around and continue north along Fifth to:

28. 35 Fifth Avenue. In 1927, Willa Cather moved to the no-longer-extant Grosvenor Hotel at 35 Fifth Avenue, today an NYU student residence.

Continue uptown on Fifth and make a right on 11th Street. The handsome town house at:

29. 21 East 11th Street was the residence of Mary Cadwaller Jones, who was married to Edith Wharton's brother. Her home was the setting of literary salons, and Henry Adams, Theodore Roosevelt, Augustus Saint-Gaudens, and John Singer Sargent often came to lunch.

Just east stands:

30. 25 East 11th Street. The unhappy and sexually confused poet Hart Crane lived here for a short time.

🔲 **REFRESHMENT STOPS** **Dean & Deluca,** 75 University Place, at 11th Street (tel. 473-1908), proffers superior light fare—pastries, croissants, ham and brie sandwiches on baguettes, pasta salads—in a pristinely charming setting enhanced by classical music. Open Monday to Thursday from 8am to 10pm, Fridays and Saturdays from 8am to 11pm, and Sundays from 9am to 8pm.

This address is also a stop on the tour. When Thomas Wolfe graduated from Harvard in 1923, he came to New York to teach at NYU and lived at the Hotel Albert (depicted as the Hotel Leopold in his novel *Of Time and the River*) at this address. Today, the Albert Apartments occupy the site.

For more substantial dining, try **Japonica,** 100 University Place, at 12th Street (tel. 243-7752), one of New York's best Japanese restaurants. Great sushi here. Open Monday to Saturday from noon to 11pm, Sundays from 1 to 10:30pm.

Double back on 11th Street toward Fifth Avenue and make a right, heading toward:

31. The Salmagundi Club, 47 Fifth Avenue, which began as an artist's club in 1871, and was originally located at 596 Broadway. The name comes from the *Salmagundi* papers, in which Washington Irving mocked his fellow New Yorkers and first used the term "Gotham" to describe the city. "Salmagundi," which means "a stew of many ingredients," was thought an appropriate term to describe the club's diverse membership—

painters, sculptors, writers, and musicians. The club moved to this old Fifth Avenue mansion in 1917. Theodore Dreiser lived at the Salmagundi in 1897 (when it was 14 West 12th Street, today the First Presbyterian Church across the street) and probably wrote *Sister Carrie* there, a work based on the experiences of his own sister, Emma.

Cross 12th Street. At the northwest corner of 12th Street and Fifth Avenue is:

32. The *Forbes* Magazine Building, housing many interesting exhibits from the varied collections of the late millionaire Malcolm Forbes—hundreds of ship models, thousands of military miniatures, bejeweled Fabergé eggs made for the czars, and more. Admission is free. Open Tuesday to Saturday from 10am to 4pm.

Make a left on 12th Street and you'll see:

33. The New School for Social Research, at 66 West 12th Street, which was founded in 1919. In the 1930s, it became a "University in Exile" for intelligentsia fleeing Nazi Germany. Many great writers have taught or lectured in its classrooms over the decades—William Styron, Joseph Heller, Edward Albee, W. H. Auden, Robert Frost, Nadine Gordimer, Max Lerner, Maya Angelou, Joyce Carol Oates, Arthur Miller, I. B. Singer, Susan Sontag, and numerous others.

Architecturally, this street between Fifth and Sixth Avenues is a delight. Turn left on Sixth to:

34. 425 Sixth Avenue. The turreted red-brick and granite Victorian-Gothic castle at this corner houses the Jefferson Market Library, built as a courthouse in 1877 and named for Thomas Jefferson. Topped by a lofty clock/bell tower (originally intended as a fire lookout), with traceried and stained-glass windows, gables, and steeply sloping roofs, the building was inspired by a Bavarian castle. In the 1880s, architects voted it one of the 10 most beautiful buildings in America. Through the early 20th century, the surrounding area comprised a market where Willa Cather used to shop for produce.

Now turn left into 10th Street, where you'll see:

35. 54 West 10th Street. Poet Hart Crane lived in this 1839 house in 1917; he paid $6 a week for rent. He was just 18 years old at the time but already published.

Across the street is:

36. 45 West 10th Street. On the site of what is today a 1950s apartment building once stood the home of Kahlil Gibran, whose work, *The Prophet,* was the rage in the 1960s. Passages from it were read at many a hippie wedding. Somehow, one can't imagine him managing to write in this present edifice.

Nearby is:

37. 50 West 10th Street. Playwright Edward Albee lived in this late 19th-century converted carriage house in the early 1960s. It's a gem of a building, with its exquisite highly polished wooden carriage doors still intact.

Now look for:

38. 37 West 10th Street. Sinclair Lewis, already a famous writer by the mid-1920s (*Main Street* and *Babbitt* were published at the beginning of the decade), lived in this early 19th-century house with his wife, journalist Dorothy Thompson, from 1928 to 1929. Lewis fell in love with Thompson at first sight in 1927, immediately proposed to her, and followed her to Russia and all over Europe until she accepted. It's a romantic story, though the marriage did end in divorce.

Our final stop is:

39. 14 West 10th Street. When Mark Twain came to New York at the turn of the century (at the age of 65), he lived in this gorgeous 1855 mansion. A greatly successful writer, he entertained lavishly.

WALKING TOUR 8

The East Village

Start: The Strand Bookstore, at the intersection of Broadway and 12th Street.
Subway: Take the 4, 5, 6, N, or R to 14th Street–Union Square station; walk south on Broadway.
Finish: Astor Place subway kiosk.
Time: 3 to 4 hours.
Best Times: Afternoons, when the neighborhood's street life begins to flash its color.
Worst Times: Although life moves at a pleasurably slow pace here on Sunday, some of the shops and churches may be closed.

Like other New York City neighborhoods, the East Village has remade itself time and time again in the years between its beginnings as part of Dutch Governor Peter Stuyvesant's farm and its current incarnation as the home of the funky fringe of the city's arts and nightlife scene. From about 1840, one immigrant enclave after another has filled the neighborhood's town houses and tenements; first Irish and German, then Italian and Jewish, and now eastern European, Japanese, and Latin American. All of these people have left their stamp here in some way, and this diversity is the East Village's defining characteristic. In the 1960s and 1970s, the neighborhood was New York's answer to San Francisco's Haight-Ashbury, home to Allen Ginsberg and Abbie Hoffman among others. Since that time it has continued to be a hub of aspiring writers, artists, and musicians.

Begin your tour at the northeast corner of Broadway and 12th Street, where you will see a beehive of activity surrounding the:

1. Strand Bookstore. This is New York City's largest used-book store. A refugee from Fourth Avenue's old Book Row (a lost mecca for the literary), the Strand has been in business for more than 60 years now and continues to be a favorite haunt of the city's rumpled intellectuals. As the store's famous slogan says, you'll find "eight miles of books" here; the main floor has used books, paperbacks, oversized art books, and review copies of new books at 50% off, downstairs is a huge selection of hardcover publisher's overstocked books, and upstairs are the collections of rare books.

Walk downtown on Broadway to 11th Street, on the northwest corner is the:

2. Cast-Iron Building. Take a look at the stately cast-iron facade of this building, with its Italian Renaissance–style columns and arches. More interesting, however, is the way the Cast-Iron Building's history typifies the changes that this part of Broadway has seen over the last 150 years. Constructed in 1868 to house the James McCreery Dry Goods Store, it is one of the few buildings left standing from the stretch of Broadway from 23rd to 8th Streets that became known after the Civil War as "Ladies Mile." Luxury hotels and elegant department stores such as McCreery's, Wanamaker's, B. Altman, and Lord and Taylor opened up in this area one after the other; by the 1870s and 1880s, the high society of New York's Gilded Age enjoyed a splendor unrivaled in the New World or even Europe. As writer Robert Macoy observed in 1876, Broadway at that time was "the grand promenade and swarm [ed] with the beauty, fashion, and wealth of New York. No avenue or street in London or Paris or Berlin, or any of our cities, can be compared with it." Toward the end of the 19th century, New York's wealthy families moved uptown, creating fashionable neighborhoods along Park, Madison, and Fifth Avenues in the 1950s, 1960s, and 1970s. Ladies Mile went into decline; when McCreery's moved uptown, the Cast-Iron Building was converted first to office and warehouse space and then in 1971 to apartments.

Across 11th Street on the southwest corner of the intersection is a lavender-colored building that used to house the:

3. St. Denis Hotel. Opened in 1848, the St. Denis for 60 years offered the pinnacle of luxury and fashion to visitors to the city. Famous guests of the hotel included Abraham Lincoln and Sarah

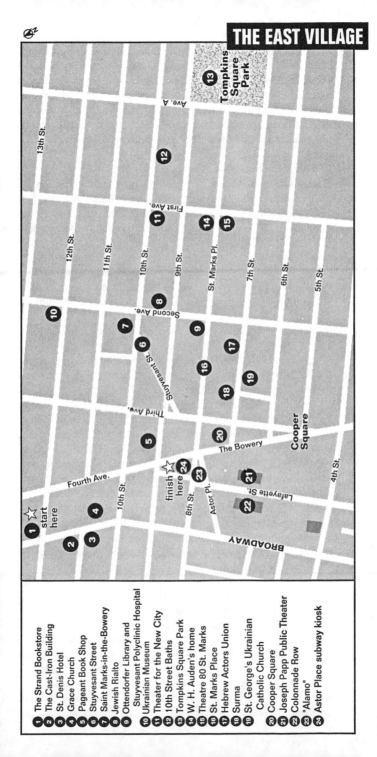

THE EAST VILLAGE

① The Strand Bookstore
② The Cast-Iron Building
③ St. Denis Hotel
④ Grace Church
⑤ Pageant Book Shop
⑥ Stuyvesant Street
⑦ Saint Marks-in-the-Bowery
⑧ Jewish Rialto
⑨ Ottendorfer Library and
   Stuyvesant Polyclinic Hospital
⑩ Ukrainian Museum
⑪ Theater for the New City
⑫ 10th Street Baths
⑬ Tompkins Square Park
⑭ W. H. Auden's home
⑮ Theatre 80 St. Marks
⑯ St. Marks Place
⑰ Hebrew Actors Union
⑱ Surma
⑲ St. George's Ukrainian
   Catholic Church
⑳ Cooper Square
㉑ Joseph Papp Public Theater
㉒ Colonnade Row
㉓ "Alamo"
㉔ Astor Place subway kiosk

Bernhardt, the eminent Parisian actress. Today the building's exterior is undistinguished; much like the Cast-Iron Building (which was robbed of its lovely mansard roof when developers replaced it with a stolid two-story addition of apartments), the St. Denis suffered injury as well as insult during Broadway's decline. All of the ornamentation that once graced the building's exterior was removed in 1917 when the St. Denis was converted to office space.

Directly across Broadway is:

4. Grace Church. One of the finest examples of Gothic Revival architecture in the United States, Grace Church was built in 1845; the adjacent rectory was completed two years later. James Renwick, Jr., who would later design Fifth Avenue's monumental St. Patrick's Cathedral, advanced his career in sacred architecture by winning a design competition held by the Protestant Episcopal church's officials. The church is nestled in a bend of Broadway, and its slender spire dramatically marks the horizon and can be seen from as many as 20 blocks south on Broadway. The exterior of the marble church and rectory features exquisitely delicate stonework and traceried stained-glass windows. Inside, you can see the fine mosaic floor, carved wood pulpit, and all the stained glass to best advantage. The church is open to the public Monday through Friday from 10am to 5:45pm and Saturdays from noon to 4pm.

If you follow the perimeter of the church grounds around to Fourth Avenue via 10th Street, you can take a look at the trio of houses built decades later in a Gothic Revival style faithful to the church itself; the northern of the trio, the Grace Memorial House, was designed by Renwick himself, whereas the two others were designed by his firm, Renwick, Aspinwall & Russell.

Ironically, despite its harmonious architecture and traditionally upper-class congregation, the most famous event to occur at Grace Church was a less than dignified one. The notorious big-top showman P. T. Barnum, ever on the lookout for sensational publicity, arranged for the nuptials of two of his "biggest" stars, the diminutive Tom Thumb and his like-sized bride Lavinia Warren, to be celebrated at the church. The 1863 wedding exhibited all of the rowdiness and hoopla that were typical of Barnum's productions.

Make your way south on Fourth Avenue. There's not much left to look at now, but 10th Street between Fourth and Third Avenues was an enormously important artists' colony in the 1950s. Abstract expressionist painters Willem and Elaine de Kooning, Philip Guston, and Esteban Vicente all had studios here, and hundreds of artists got their start at the co-op galleries that once lined both sides of the street. At 9th Street, you'll see looming over the southwest corner of Fourth Avenue and Wanamaker Place the enormous Wanamaker Department Store Annex, another cast-iron survivor from Ladies Mile; it has been reduced to housing the city's Parking Violations Bureau. Turn east onto 9th Street. On your left is the:

5. **Pageant Book Shop,** at 109 9th Street. This charming second-hand bookstore has been in business since 1945, located first uptown and then at several Fourth Avenue Book Row locations before moving to its current home in 1978. Downstairs you'll find its rare books and its wonderful print and map collection. Both the cluttered second-hand hardcover and paperback departments upstairs and the shop's royal-blue storefront will be familiar to film buffs because they are among the settings used in Woody Allen's 1986 film *Hannah and Her Sisters*—one of his love letters to New York.

Continue east across Third Avenue on 9th Street. This block of 9th Street has recently become known as one of the city's "Little Japans"; it boasts a Japanese hair salon, art supply store, video store, three sushi restaurants, and downstairs at no. 240 is the city's first karaoke bar, Candy-B1. Bear left onto:

6. **Stuyvesant Street.** This street is the namesake of the last Dutch governor of New York City, Peter Stuyvesant. "Peg Leg Peter," a dour colonial governor, built a large *bouwerie,* or farm, for himself on the surrounding land in the mid-1600s, siting his house at the intersection of Stuyvesant and 10th Streets. His descendants continued to reside in the area into the 19th century. Number 21, known as the Stuyvesant-Fish House, is one such residence, built in 1804 by the governor's great-grandson as a wedding gift to his daughter. When city officials decided in 1811 to impose the street grid that characterizes Manhattan today, the wealthy families here saved the street from being razed; it is one of the few true east-west streets left in the city. Adjacent to the Stuyvesant-Fish House begins the Renwick Triangle, a group of 16 ivy-covered brick-and-brownstone houses built in 1861 at the tip of the intersection of Stuyvesant and East 10th Streets by the aforementioned James Renwick.

At the end of Stuyvesant Street, across 10th Street, is:

7. **Saint Marks-in-the-Bowery.** This Episcopal church stands on the oldest site of a house of worship in the city—built in 1799, it replaced the 1660 chapel that was part of Peter Stuyvesant's farm. To the left and right of the portico are statues of Native Americans by Solon Borglum, and busts of Stuyvesant and Daniel Tompkins, who banned slavery from New York City. Stuyvesant's remains are interred in one of the odd-shaped brick burial vaults in the ivy-covered courtyard, as are those of a number of prominent 18th- and 19th-century New Yorkers. You

can get a look at the church's Georgian interior Monday to Friday from 9am to 4pm. Saint Marks-in-the-Bowery has ardently supported the arts community in the East Village for years; two long-running church programs are Danspace and the Poetry Project. Beat poet Allen Ginsberg and avant-garde playwright Sam Shepard have often read at the latter, which continues to present new poets and writers such as David Trinidad, Jim Carroll, and Darius James.

REFRESHMENT STOPS Bordering the east side of Saint Marks-in-the-Bowery is Second Avenue, which from 14th to Houston Streets is lined with a wildly eclectic array of restaurants and nightspots, many of which still reflect the traditions of the neighborhood's immigrant enclaves. One is the **Ukrainian Restaurant,** located just below East 9th Street at 140 Second Avenue, right in the center of the area's Ukrainian community. The dining room exudes a warm, homey charm, and the menu features eastern European specialties such as pierogi, potato pancakes, stuffed cabbage, borscht, and a delicious tripe soup.

And on the southeast corner of Second Avenue and East 10th Street is the **Second Avenue Deli,** which gets my vote as New York's best kosher deli. A neighborhood institution in business for over 30 years, it serves up Jewish soul food nonpareil—chopped liver, kasha varnishkes, knishes, incredible soups that regulars swear will cure the common cold, and great pastrami and corned beef sandwiches. The fast-talking waiters will engage you in some Borscht Belt banter, and the latest news from Wall Street blinks across the restaurant's stock ticker.

It won't be easy in either of these stick-to-your-ribs emporia, but try and leave some room for a special coffee and dessert stop not far ahead.

Stop in front of Second Avenue Deli's portal after your meal. The brass stars set into the sidewalk commemorate Second Avenue's heyday as the:

8. Jewish Rialto. New York's Jewish community increased in number and prosperity in the early years of the 20th century, and the new Jewish middle class turned Second Avenue into a center of Yiddish culture, bristling with cafés, bookstores, and a score of Yiddish-language theaters. The Jewish Rialto peaked in the 1920s as actors such as Jacob Adler, Paul Muni, and Maurice Schwartz took the stage every night in plays usually portraying a sentimental "immigrant-makes-good" theme. Very little trace of this era remains, but many of the theaters—such as the Yiddish Arts Theatre on 12th Street and Second Avenue (now a multiscreen movie theater) and the Orpheum on Second Avenue south of St. Marks Place (still staging plays) are still here.

Across Second Avenue from the Ukrainian Restaurant is the:

9. **Ottendorfer Library and Stuyvesant Polyclinic Hospital.** These two facilities are the 1884 gift of Anna and Oswald Ottendorfer, publishers of a German language daily newspaper, to the once-thriving German community of this neighborhood. The library, a branch of the New York City Public Library, is adorned with terra-cotta globes, books, owls, and a German inscription; the adjacent clinic features portrait busts of Hippocrates, Celsius, Humboldt, Linnaeus, and other scientists and physicians. Ottendorfer himself selected the library's original collection; the library has kept up with the changing character of the neighborhood by adding Polish, Ukrainian, French, Chinese, and Spanish books to its shelves. The clinic was originally named the German Dispensary; its administrators attempted to deflect strong anti-German sentiment during the world wars by changing its name to the Stuyvesant Polyclinic Hospital, and the name has stuck ever since.

Walk north on Second Avenue past 12th Street. Look for no. 203 on your left; upstairs in this building is the:

10. **Ukrainian Museum.** This small museum is committed to preserving the cultural heritage of the thousands of Ukrainian Americans who live in the East Village and elsewhere. On permanent display are an assortment of folk art items, including traditional Ukrainian clothing; *pysanky*, or intricately decorated Easter eggs; *rushnyky*, ritual cloths that play a number of important functions in Ukrainian society; and decorative ceramics and brass and silver jewelry. The museum also has a growing fine arts collection and stages frequent special exhibits.

Backtrack on Second Avenue to its intersection with 11th Street and turn left.

REFRESHMENT STOPS The intersection of First Avenue and 11th Street is the heart of what remains of a small Italian community. A number of bakeries and delis here purvey Old World staples, but the real treasures of the area are a pair of pastry shops. Walking down 11th Street, it would be hard not to notice the milling crowds of patrons and gleaming brass fixtures of **Veniero's,** a famous establishment that draws visitors from all over for its exquisite pastries and cakes. More bang for the buck, however, can be had at **De Robertis'**

Pastry Shop at 176 First Avenue. The cannoli and cappuccino are every bit as good, and the café's friendly confines draw loyal local patrons who lounge for hours on end in the large comfortable booths. Legend has it that De Robertis' marvelous tile and mosaic interior was the work of an off-duty Italian subway mason—it *does* somehow remind you of an IRT subway station.

Walk south on First Avenue to 10th Street. Just past the southwest corner of the intersection is the:

11. Theater for the New City. After 21 seasons presenting cutting-edge drama, poetry, music, dance, and the visual arts, the TNC's productions remain eclectic, politically engaged, fearless, multicultural, and above all, furiously creative. Stop in and pick up a program.

Cross First Avenue and walk east on 10th Street. On your right in the middle of the block is an unusual institution, the:

12. 10th Street Baths. There were once many Turkish-style bathhouses in New York City; some of them, such as the Coney Island baths and the Luxor on 42nd Street, became the famous, or at least notorious, hangouts of gangsters and celebrities. This place is the last of them; as such, it is the sole repository of a fascinating—some might say downright weird—tradition. The regular patrons, Russian immigrants and Orthodox Jews, come here for a *schvitz,* Yiddish for "sweat." In the Russian Room, where 11 tons of red-hot rocks raise the temperature to a scalding 300°F, they sit, occasionally dumping a bucket of ice water over their heads. Occasionally, they ask an attendant (in the old days a deaf-mute incapable of following the conversations of the mobsters) for a *platzka,* a scrubbing with a bristled brush made of oak leaves. Afterward, the bathers flop into an ice-cold pool, wrap themselves in a pink robe, and head upstairs for some more talk and an old-fashioned meal of borscht, whitefish salad, kasha, and the like as well as a few shots of frozen vodka. One man who has visited the baths several times a week for 75 years summed up his loyalty to the place: "When I walk out from here, I am like a newborn baby. . . . Why should I deny myself this little pleasure?"

Tenth Street next intersects with the first of the "Alphabet City" thoroughfares, Avenue A. Opening up from the southeast corner of the intersection is:

13. Tompkins Square Park. In its own way, this 16-acre park is as much a focal point of the East Village as famed Washington Square is of Greenwich Village proper. However, while Washington Square attracts throngs of tourists, Tompkins Square remains a true neighborhood park. Its fresh air and open spaces attract everyone who lives in the cramped tenements that surround the park for blocks on every side.

The Slavic teenagers who staff the newsstand/soda fountain facing the park near the corner of Avenue A and 7th Street make great chocolate and vanilla egg creams—the traditional drink of the Lower East Side. Get yourself one and head into the park at the 9th Street entrance.

Tompkins Square began as a salt marsh known as Stuyvesant Swamp; the Stuyvesant family gave the land to the city in 1833. About halfway across the 9th Street walkway into the park and through a brick portico is an eroded monument that commemorates a tragedy that was a swan song of sorts for the first immigrants to put their stamp on this area, the Germans. In 1904 the passenger ferry *General Slocum* sank in the East River with 1,200 aboard, most of whom were women and children from "Dutchtown" ("Dutch" being here a corruption of *Deutsch*) in the East Village. Many of the survivors found it impossible to continue living in the East Village after this disaster and moved to other German neighborhoods in the city, but the German community's legacy lives on in the solid middle-class houses that stand on the north side of the square and on the streets running from Second Avenue to the park.

Follow the park's walkways toward the southwest and you'll see the Temperance Fountain, built in 1888 in hopes of convincing the thirsty to choose water over alcoholic spirits. At the southwest corner of the park is a statue of Congressman Samuel Cox, the "Postman's Friend," whose efforts to increase salaries and improve working conditions in the U.S. Postal Service made him a sort of patron saint of letter carriers.

One of the more interesting historical byways of this neighborhood and the rest of the Lower East Side is the frequency with which the area has become a battleground between the city's monied interests and the poor immigrant communities that it has housed. In the 19th and early 20th centuries, Tompkins Square often functioned as a venue for socialist and labor rallies. In 1874, one such gathering was violently dispersed by city police, an event that became known as the Tompkins Square Massacre. Tensions in recent years have centered on the real estate industry's attempts to gentrify the neighborhood; local frustration with escalating rents came to a head in 1988 when police attempted to enforce a curfew in the park and an ugly riot ensued. The Christodora House, a 17-story building that looms over the eastern edge of the park, came to symbolize the recent conflict. The Christodora House was built in 1928 as a settlement house and for many years was an important community and social service center. To the dismay of area residents, in 1987 developers converted it to high-priced condominiums; vandals did extensive damage to the building on the night of the riot. The neighborhood has, however, been calm for the most part since then, and the extensive renovations made to the park in 1992 have been welcomed by most residents.

Leave the park on the Avenue A side and stroll west along St. Marks Place. Just across First Avenue on the north side of the street is:

14. W. H. Auden's home, at 77 St. Marks Place. Auden lived and worked on the third floor here for two decades until 1972, shortly before his death. Although Auden generally kept a low profile in the neighborhood, he was a parishioner at Saint Marks-in-the-Bowery and occasionally drank at the bar that still occupies the basement level of the adjoining building; you can still find a newspaper clipping or two about Auden on the windows and walls of local shops. Earlier in the century, the Russian Communist periodical *Novy Mir,* to which Leon Trotsky often contributed, was printed here.

Across the street is:

15. Theatre 80 St. Marks. New York's revival cinemas always seem to have a too-short lifespan, but this one has been here for many years. Proprieter Howard Otway cooks up dream double features every day, and the theater itself is more or less a shrine to the silver screen, with pictures of matinee idols of the thirties, forties, and fifties hung about like oracles. Candy, brownies, and coffee are served over an old speakeasy bar.

Follow this street west and you will soon reach the surreal center of the East Village counterculture:

16. St. Marks Place, between Second and Third Avenues. The upper-class origins of this block (still faintly discernible in the 19th-century town houses at nos. 4, 6, and 20) have been largely obscured by a 25-year reign of hippies, punks, and various street people who defy categorization. The block has at this point declined to a state of general seediness, but a walk up and back on these sidewalks is definitely interesting. On the north side of the street at midblock is the All-Craft Self-Help Center, around which a crowd is almost always gathered. Before its current incarnation as a community center, it was home to such legendary nightclubs as the psychedelic Electric Circus and Andy Warhol's Exploding Plastic Inevitable. The rest of the block is lined with stores ranging from St. Marks Books (a mainstay of the local left-wing intelligentsia) to Trash and Vaudeville (in which aspiring rock stars can find vintage clothing, leather jackets, and combat boots) to numerous tawdry souvenir shops.

Make your way back to Second Avenue and turn right, then turn right again onto 7th Street. On the north side of the street at no. 31, look up for the granite facade, into which is carved the name of the:

17. Hebrew Actors Union. During the heyday of Yiddish theater on Second Avenue, even the biggest stars used to pay regular visits to this building. Today, despite the almost total demise of Yiddish theater in the neighborhood, the union is still active.

REFRESHMENT STOP One of the few vestiges of the days when the East Village had a significant Irish community, **McSorley's Old Ale House and Grill,** 15 East 7th Street (tel. 473-9148), established in 1854, is New York's oldest watering hole. It looks—and smells—every bit its age; toward the back an old potbellied stove radiates heat, and a thicket of photos, newspaper clippings, and various knick-knacks that only a regular could know the meaning of hang from the walls, all gone yellow and brown with age and a century's worth of tobacco smoke. Over the years, luminaries from Peter Cooper to Brendan Behan have earned the right to a particular chair or bar stool, and the bar's beery charm was captured in Joseph Mitchell's *New Yorker* stories, since collected in a book, *McSorley's Wonderful Saloon.* Perhaps the only significant change McSorley's has undergone in this century occurred in 1970, when a group of women successfully challenged its men-only policy. If you drop in on an afternoon for a drink and simple fare—beer, sandwiches, chili, and raw onions are about all you'll choose from—you might just catch a glimpse of the New York that Peter Cooper knew. But come here on Friday or Saturday night, and you'll be forced to jostle with a boisterous, beer-swilling college crowd.

McSorley's is really an anachronism on 7th Street these days, which is now the heart of a Ukrainian immigrant community some 20,000 strong. Known as Little Ukraine, it boasts:

18. Surma, a store at no. 11 that seems to function partly as a community center. Ukrainian newspapers and books and eastern European handcrafts—intricately embroidered peasant blouses (which Karen Allen wore as Harrison Ford's costar in the film *Raiders of the Lost Ark*), paintings, traditional porcelain, dolls, and *pysanky* (decorated eggs)—are featured here. According to legend, *pysanky* conquer evil, and only if enough eggs are painted will the forces of good triumph. So buy an egg-decorating kit and get busy.

Across the street, on the east side of Taras Shevchenko Place, is:

19. St. George's Ukrainian Catholic Church. It is elaborately decorated inside and out with mosaic tilework, and its dome is adorned with 16 beautiful stained-glass windows. This church was completed in 1977, and its modest predecessor was recently torn down to allow the adjoining large, brand-new rectory to be built. Together they testify to the growing wealth and vitality of Little Ukraine.

Across Third Avenue from 7th Street is:

20. Cooper Square. Situated on this triangular lot are the Cooper Union Foundation Building and a small park with a templelike structure housing a bronze likeness of Peter Cooper (1791–1883), an inventor, industrialist, and philanthropist, and one of the great geniuses of his day. He made the bulk of his fortune through an ironworks and a glue factory, built the first steam locomotive in the United States, the *Tom Thumb,* developed the first rolled-steel railroad rails, and was instrumental in laying the first transatlantic telegraph cable. Cooper, a self-educated man from modest roots, believed that his wealth carried with it a responsibility to improve the working man's situation, and so he founded the Cooper Union to provide free education in the practical trades and arts to any man or woman who wished to attend. A sense of Cooper as a benevolent, fatherly figure flows from the statue, and it's only natural: the sculptor, Augustus Saint-Gaudens, was able to attend Cooper Union's art school because of its founder's characteristic generosity.

The Cooper Union Foundation Building was completed in 1859. It was the first building in New York to use wrought-iron beams (another Cooper innovation), the forerunners of the steel I-beams that are the skeleton of present-day skyscrapers. The Italianate brownstone exterior remains much as it was in the 19th century. The interior, however, underwent extensive renovations in 1975 at the hands of John Hejduk, dean of Cooper Union's architecture school; the results add considerably to the building's appeal. Enter the building and go to the rear of the lobby to see an elaborate and amusing carved-wood birthday card given to the founder by the senior class of 1871, thanking him for his 80th-birthday gift of $150,000 to the school. A staircase in the lobby leads down to the Great Hall; in keeping with Peter Cooper's designs for it, the Great Hall has functioned over the years as a free public forum in which great issues of the day are debated. Labor leader Samuel Gompers, free-love advocate Victoria Woodhull, and Sioux chief Red Cloud all spoke here, but perhaps the Great Hall's most famous moment occurred in 1860, when Abraham Lincoln's fiery "right makes might" antislavery speech carried public opinion in New York and sped him to the Republican Party's presidential nomination.

Walk around the Cooper Union and turn left onto Peltier Street, then hang another left onto Lafayette Street, which in the 1850s was the city's most elegant residential boulevard. A few paces down on your left is the:

21. **Joseph Papp Public Theater.** The Public, one of New York's most vital cultural institutions, is housed in the old Astor Library. This red-brick palazzo, the first public library in New York City, was the lone public bequest of John Jacob Astor, who made millions in the fur trade and was a notoriously tightfisted landowner. In 1911 the library's collection was moved to the New York Public Library on 42nd Street. From 1920 to 1966, the Hebrew Immigrant Aid Society used the building to shelter and feed thousands of Jewish immigrants and help them gain a footing in the United States. When they moved elsewhere, city officials and Joseph Papp's New York Shakespeare Festival rescued the Astor Library from a developer who had planned to raze it to make way for an apartment complex; the building was designated a city landmark and became the permanent indoor home of the New York Shakespeare Festival.

    The Public Theater opened in 1967 with the original production of *Hair,* which moved on to Broadway; in 1975 *A Chorus Line* followed suit, becoming the longest-running show in Broadway history. Over the years, the New York Shakespeare Festival has presented on the Public's five stages new plays by such major playwrights as David Rabe, John Guare, David Mamet, Caryl Churchill, and Larry Kramer. Founder Joseph Papp died in 1992, but the theater continues to thrive, with cinema offerings, poetry readings, lectures, a café, a bookstore, and a late-night cabaret added to its offerings. A show here makes for a wonderful evening; unsold tickets are often available as half-price "Quiktix" after 6pm (1pm for matinees on Saturday and Sunday) in the lobby.

    Across the street from the Public Theater is:

22. **Colonnade Row,** a group of row houses fronted by a crumbling marble colonnade. Of the nine row houses built by developer Seth Geer in 1831, only four remain; the five on the south end were demolished to make room for the Wanamaker Department Store warehouse. When built, these houses were fronted by 30-foot gardens and Lafayette Street was a quiet, posh residential district; John Jacob Astor lived here, as did members of the Vanderbilt and Delano families and writer Washington Irving. The fashionable set moved uptown after the Civil War and these houses have been in decline ever since, but if

you look at the roof of no. 434 (the Astor Place Theater is on the ground floor), you'll see the carved-stone honeysuckle-leaf border that once stretched across all nine houses.

Turn back and walk toward Astor Place. The black metal sculpture that dominates the traffic island in the middle of the intersection is the:

23. "Alamo," known universally to area residents as "the Cube." Sculptor Tony Rosenthal built the piece in 1967 for a city-sponsored exhibition. He is reportedly pleased that the "Alamo" has become a participatory piece—it was built on a rotating post so that it could be positioned after installation, but it has become a tradition in the East Village for anyone feeling a bit rowdy to spin the Cube.

The next and last stop is on the adjoining traffic island across 8th Street, the:

24. Astor Place subway kiosk. Earlier in this century, almost every IRT subway stop in Manhattan had a kiosk much like this one. The Transit Authority inexplicably decided to tear them all down in 1911, but when the Astor Place subway station was restored in 1985, officials revived what had been a lost element of New York City's architectural scene. (Down in the station, Milton Glaser's mosaics and the ceramic low-relief tiles depicting beavers—the animal whose pelt made John Jacob Astor's fortune—are definitely worth a look.) And Peter Cooper would no doubt have been deeply satisfied to know that the architect of the new kiosk was a Cooper Union graduate.

WALKING TOUR 9

Midtown

Start: Grand Central Station.
Subway: Take the 4, 5, 6, or the shuttle to 42nd Street/Grand Central.
Finish: The Museum of Modern Art.
Time: Approximately 3 hours, not counting time for browsing in shops and galleries.
Best Times: Weekdays, when Midtown is bustling but the attractions aren't packed with crowds of tourists.
Worst Times: Rush hour (weekdays from 8:30 to 9:30am and from 4:30 to 6pm).

If there's an area that's unmistakably New York, it's Midtown. Concentrated here are dozens of the towering skyscrapers that are so closely identified with the city and its skyline; as you walk past them, craning your neck upward in awe, you'll be jostled by crowds of the office workers who occupy these mammoth edifices. Lining Fifth Avenue and 57th Street are blue-chip art galleries, plus the high-toned boutiques and chic department stores that make New York the consumer capital of the world. Midtown is Manhattan at its most glamorous.

From the subway platform, follow the Metro North signs to the main concourse of:

1. Grand Central Station. Commodore Vanderbilt himself

named the place "Grand Central" in the 1860s, notwithstanding the fact that it was then out in the boondocks. The original station underwent more or less continuous alterations until the present structure replaced it in 1913. Besides being visually magnificent, it's an engineering tour de force, combining subways, surface streets, pedestrian malls, underground shopping concourses, and 48 pairs of railroad tracks together with attendant platforms and concourses into one smoothly functioning organism.

The main concourse is perfectly breathtaking. It's one of America's most impressive interior spaces—125 feet high, 375 feet long, and 120 feet wide—and it boasts fine stone carvings, gleaming marble floors, and sweeping staircases. Don't forget to look up—the blue vaulted ceiling is decorated with constellations of twinkling stars.

Leave the main concourse via the 42nd Street exit and look up; looming over you is the sleek art deco:

2. **Chrysler Building.** At 1,048 feet, it reigned briefly as the tallest building in the world—until the Empire State Building came along. Notice the huge winged radiator caps that mark the base of the tower. The Chrysler Building's spire is one of the most distinctive features of the Manhattan skyline; you can't see it when you're this close, but you'll get a good view of it later in our tour.

Head west along 42nd Street. Make a left onto Fifth Avenue, where the:

3. **New York Public Library** sits in majestic splendor. Climb up the broad stone steps in front, which are flanked by two stone lions named "Patience" and "Fortitude." Completed in 1911, this beaux arts palace cost over $9 million, and President Taft himself attended the dedication ceremony. The sumptuous interior is well worth exploring; you'll find millions of volumes occupying more than 80 miles of bookshelves.

Now start walking uptown on the west side of Fifth Avenue and look up—you'll get a wonderful perspective on the Chrysler Building. Continue north for a couple of blocks to 44th Street, where you'll turn left. On the north side of 44th, at no. 27, is the **New York Harvard Club,** designed by McKim, Mead and White in 1894 in an architectural style that was favored in the late 1800s at Harvard.

Continue along 44th Street. Near Sixth Avenue stands one of New York's most famous literary shrines:

4. **The Algonquin Hotel.** In the hotel bar, the members of the legendary Round Table held forth—James Thurber, George Kaufman, Robert Benchley, and of course the inimitable and formidable Dorothy Parker, book critic for the *New Yorker.*

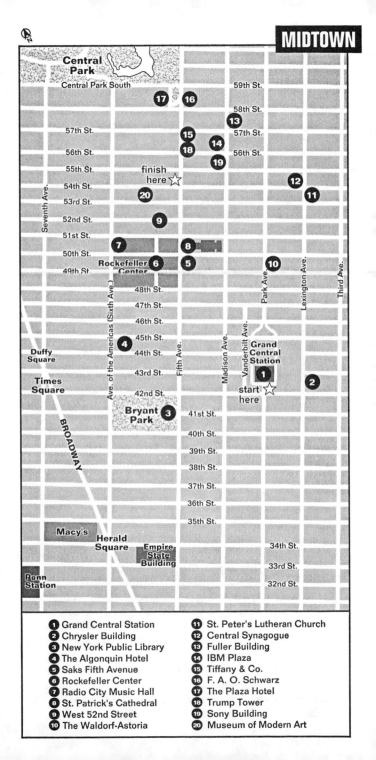

MIDTOWN

Central Park

Central Park South

59th St.
58th St.
57th St.
56th St.
55th St.

finish here ☆

Seventh Ave.

Rockefeller Center

Ave. of the Americas (Sixth Ave.)

Fifth Ave.

Madison Ave.

Vanderbilt Ave.

Park Ave.

Lexington Ave.

Third Ave.

Duffy Square

Times Square

BROADWAY

Bryant Park

Grand Central Station

start here ☆

Macy's

Herald Square

Empire State Building

Penn Station

① Grand Central Station
② Chrysler Building
③ New York Public Library
④ The Algonquin Hotel
⑤ Saks Fifth Avenue
⑥ Rockefeller Center
⑦ Radio City Music Hall
⑧ St. Patrick's Cathedral
⑨ West 52nd Street
⑩ The Waldorf-Astoria

⑪ St. Peter's Lutheran Church
⑫ Central Synagogue
⑬ Fuller Building
⑭ IBM Plaza
⑮ Tiffany & Co.
⑯ F. A. O. Schwarz
⑰ The Plaza Hotel
⑱ Trump Tower
⑲ Sony Building
⑳ Museum of Modern Art

The movers and shakers in the publishing world today are more likely to be found in the lobby bar of the futuristic **Royalton Hotel** just across the street. Poke your head in and take a look—the decor, created by designer Phillippe Starck, has to be seen to be believed.

Retrace your steps back to Fifth Avenue and head north. Take a detour to your left when you pass 47th Street. This block, between Fifth and Sixth Avenues, is the **Diamond District,** where every day hundreds of millions of dollars' worth of diamonds are traded. Peer into a few of the shop windows and you'll see dazzling gems on display.

Continue up Fifth Avenue toward 49th Street; on the right side of the avenue stands one of New York's legendary department stores:

5. Saks Fifth Avenue. Step inside for a few minutes and browse through the chic designer clothes and accessories; you'll be caught up in a very well-heeled crowd of shoppers.

Now head west into the promenade of:

6. Rockefeller Center, one of the most handsome urban complexes in New York, perhaps in the nation. It encompasses 24 acres and 19 skyscrapers, extending from 47th to 52nd Streets between Fifth and Sixth Avenues.

As you stroll west, you'll encounter the Channel Gardens, with their beautiful plantings, before you arrive at Rockefeller Center's famous skating rink. In winter it's packed with skaters gliding along the ice, while music wafts through the air and the trees surrounding the rink are lit with twinkling lights. Around the rink flutter the colorful flags of nations from around the world. Each holiday season a giant Christmas tree stands here, towering over the promenade. Paul Manship's massive golden statue of *Prometheus* sits above the skating rink, beneath a quote from Aeschylus: "Prometheus teacher in every art brought the fire that hath proven to mortals means to mighty ends."

Take a look inside the lobby of 30 Rockefeller Plaza. Above the black marble floors and walls are monumental sepia-toned murals by José María Sert. Originally, a highly political mural by Diego Rivera faced the building's front door. Rather than remove an image of Lenin hovering over a tableau of rich people playing cards, Rivera insisted the mural be destroyed. The Rockefellers willingly obliged.

Just to the left of 30 Rockefeller Plaza is 49th Street; take it and head west to Sixth Avenue. You'll pass the entrance to NBC Studios (where *Late Night with David Letterman* was taped for many years before Letterman defected to CBS) and to the Rainbow Room, one of New York's most glamorous supper clubs.

When you reach Sixth Avenue, turn right and start heading uptown. A building boom in the 1960s and 1970s transformed this area into an astonishing canyon of 50-story glass skyscrapers. Although this is just another Manhattan business district and the buildings individually aren't of great note, taken together they form an urban environment of considerable grandeur.

On the right side of Sixth Avenue, north of 50th Street, stands:

7. **Radio City Music Hall,** which has been restored to its 1930s art deco elegance. Its shows run the gamut from the annual Christmas Spectacular—starring Radio City's own Rockettes—to performances by stars like Liza Minelli. Guided tours are available; call 247-4777 for information.

Now retrace your steps through the Rockefeller Center complex and walk east, crossing Fifth Avenue. Between 50th and 51st Streets is:

8. **St. Patrick's Cathedral,** the seat of the Archdiocese of New York. Designed by James Renwick, it's a magnificent Gothic-style structure, with twin spires rising 330 feet above street level. Zelda and F. Scott Fitzgerald were married here in 1920, and stayed at the nearby Biltmore Hotel (which has since been demolished) on their honeymoon—that is, until they proved a bit too rowdy for the management and were asked to leave.

Continue uptown on Fifth toward 52nd Street. Take a look to your left, where:

9. **West 52nd Street** has been designated "Swing Street." You'd never know it just by looking, but this block holds a special place in jazz history. It was lined with a number of illicit speakeasies during Prohibition, and after its repeal, many of the establishments became jazz clubs, nurturing such great talents as Billie Holiday, Fats Waller, Dizzy Gillespie, Charlie Parker, and Sarah Vaughan.

The **Twenty-one Club,** at 21 West 52nd, is still a popular restaurant and one of the few establishments to survive from this era. (Operating as a speakeasy during Prohibition, it relied on several clever devices to guard against police raids, such as a trap door on the bar that sent everyone's cocktails tumbling into the sewer when a button was pressed.)

Now retrace your steps on 52nd Street and head east. Make a right onto Park Avenue, where, at 50th Street, you'll see one of the most famous hotels in the world:

10. **The Waldorf-Astoria.** Cole Porter and his wife lived here for many years, in one of the permanent apartments in the Waldorf Towers; one of the hotel's dining spots, Peacock Alley, still boasts his piano. Other famous residents of these luxury suites have included Gen. Douglas MacArthur, Herbert Hoover,

Henry and Clare Booth Luce, and the Duke and Duchess of Windsor. Gangster Lucky Luciano also lived here under an alias until he was forced to leave the Waldorf for less luxurious digs—in the state penitentiary.

Take 50th Street east to Lexington Avenue and turn left, heading north.

REFRESHMENT STOPS At 53rd Street and Lexington Avenue stands **Citicorp Center.** If you enter and head downstairs to the plaza level, you'll find café tables scattered under the atrium for those who want to grab a frozen yogurt, a salad, or a sandwich.

There are several more formal restaurants here, too, including **La Brochette** for French fare, **Alfredo** for Italian cuisine, and my favorite spot, **Avgerinos,** a Greek café with sparkling white walls that are decorated with brightly colored pottery. Main courses, which run under $15, include such traditional Greek favorites as chicken souvlaki, roast leg of lamb, moussaka, and stuffed grape leaves. Top off your main course with the baklava.

At the southeast corner of 54th Street and Lexington Avenue stands:

11. St. Peter's Lutheran Church, a modern structure built in 1977 and adorned with sculptures by Louise Nevelson. St. Peter's is famous for its Sunday evening Jazz Vespers, where many of the greatest names in jazz have performed. Look through the window facing Lexington Avenue to get a glimpse of the striking, almost stark interior.

Just north of St. Peter's at 55th Street is the:

12. Central Synagogue, one of New York's finest examples of Moorish-Revival-style architecture. The oldest synagogue building in continuous use in the city, it was dedicated in 1870.

Just a couple of blocks uptown, you'll turn left onto 57th Street, which is home to many of the city's established art galleries and upscale boutiques. (Stop and browse whenever you see a gallery that looks intriguing.) Heading west, you'll come to the beautiful art deco:

13. Fuller Building at the northeast corner of Madison Avenue and 57th Street. Look at the bronze doors, the marble fixtures, and mosaic walls—and plan to spend some time investigating the many galleries housed here.

On the downtown side of 57th Street, just west of Madison Avenue, is the:

14. IBM Plaza. Walking west, you'll pass the IBM Gallery of Science and Art, which is full of interactive exhibits; admission is free. Just beyond the gallery is an entrance to IBM's atrium; inside is nothing less than a glass-enclosed bamboo forest. It's a great place to sit and have a light snack from the refreshment kiosk (though it's crowded at lunchtime). There are tables and chairs, fascinating aromatic plantings that change with the seasons, and an impressive sense of space. If you're fortunate, there may even be a little concert (chamber music or some such) in progress beneath the bamboos. IBM deserves high marks for this one.

Continue west on 57th Street; when you reach Fifth Avenue, you'll see one of the most famous retail stores in Manhattan:

15. Tiffany & Co., with its windows full of amazing gems and glittering trinkets. (Who could forget Audrey Hepburn as Holly Golightly, gracefully strolling by these same windows in *Breakfast at Tiffany's?*) Go in and look at the display cases; you'll probably see a few customers here choosing engagement rings.

Head uptown on Fifth Avenue, passing one of the priciest stores in Manhattan's retail world, Bergdorf Goodman. Just north of 58th Street is one of the most delightful places in all of Manhattan:

16. F.A.O. Schwarz, the toy store of every child's dreams. You may remember Tom Hanks's famous dance interpretation of "Chopsticks," performed on a giant piano keyboard in the movie *Big*. The stuffed animal department on the first floor is my favorite section; it's a jungle full of cuddly lions, tigers, and bears. Allow plenty of time to browse through this wonderland of toys.

Across from F.A.O. Schwarz stands the landmark:

17. Plaza Hotel, built in 1907. F. Scott Fitzgerald once made a splash (literally) in the fountain in front of the hotel, when he dove right in; he also used the Plaza as one of the settings in his masterpiece, *The Great Gatsby*. Another famous guest, Frank Lloyd Wright, stayed in a suite overlooking the park while he designed the Guggenheim Museum. Young visitors will be familiar with the Plaza as the heroine's home in the children's classic *Eloise*.

Double back on Fifth Avenue, heading downtown again. Just below Tiffany's on the east side of Fifth Avenue, between 56th and 57th Streets, is the entrance to:

18. Trump Tower. This glittery mixed-use cooperative, developed by The Donald himself, has commercial tenants on the lower floors and million-dollar-plus apartments upstairs. Push the huge gold Ts mounted on the doors and you'll enter a posh shopping atrium with a showy 80-foot waterfall and more pink marble than you would have supposed existed in all of Italy.

After a few exhilarating breaths of Mr. Trump's world, exit and take 56th Street east to Madison Avenue and Philip Johnson's:

19. Sony Building. Opened in 1983, this post-modern structure (formerly the A T & T Building) has a facade of pink granite and a distinctive top that resembles a notched piece of Chippendale furniture.

Head down to 55th Street and make a right, returning to Fifth Avenue.

REFRESHMENT STOP   There's no better place to stop for an afternoon cocktail than the bar where the Bloody Mary was invented—the **King Cole Bar and Lounge,** housed in the St. Regis Hotel, 2 East 55th Street. Don't forget to admire the mural of Old King Cole. (There's also an elegant afternoon tea served in the Astor Court, which boasts a vaulted ceiling, trompe-l'oeil cloud murals, and exquisite 22-karat gold leafing.)

The hotel itself is a landmark, built in 1904 by John Jacob Astor and housing some of the most expensive, opulent rooms in the city. Ernest Hemingway, Alfred Hitchcock, and Salvador Dalí all stayed at the St. Regis, and John Lennon and Yoko Ono occupied suites here in the early seventies.

Take Fifth Avenue downtown to 53rd Street and make a right. Here stands one of New York's top attractions, the:

20. Museum of Modern Art, which offers an unrivaled survey of the arts from 1880 to the present. You can explore the development of modern art in more than 20 galleries, viewing masterpieces like van Gogh's *Starry Night* and Picasso's *Les Demoiselles d'Avignon,* one of the most important works in the cubist movement. Films—mainly by international and American independent filmmakers—are shown daily in the museum's two theaters. My favorite part of the museum is the Abby Aldrich Rockefeller Sculpture Garden, which contains works by Rodin and Nevelson, as well as Picasso's charming *The Goat.*

You might want to save MOMA for another time and devote a whole day to really exploring its thousands of treasures. If you do want to enter, you should know that the museum is open on Thursdays from 11am to 8:45pm; Friday through Tuesday from 11am to 5:45pm. Admission is charged.

You don't have to pay the admission charge, however, to

browse in MOMA's bookstore, which offers a wonderful selection of art books. Just across the street is MOMA's design store, where you can take a look at the latest trends in housewares—there's exquisite glassware, flatware, and pottery, plus an eclectic array of gadgetry from clocks to garden shears.

―――――

Central Park

―――――

Start: Grand Army Plaza, at 59th Street and Fifth Avenue.
Subway: Take the N or R to Fifth Avenue.
Finish: The Vanderbilt Gate, the entrance to the Conservatory
Garden, at 105th Street and Fifth Avenue.
Time: Approximately 5 hours, including lunch. If you want to
explore more fully (stopping to visit the zoo for an hour or two, for
instance), consider breaking up this tour into a two-day excursion.
Best Times: Weekends, weather permitting, when the park hums
with activity.

Central Park was designed by landscape architects par excellence
Frederick Law Olmsted and Calvert Vaux in the late 1850s, when
its land was still on the outskirts of the city. Its advent ensured that
New Yorkers would always have recourse to pastoral tranquillity.
One of the world's most beautiful urban parks, it's a recreational
greenbelt of woodlands, wisteria-shaded arbors, duck- and swan-
filled lakes and lagoons, meadows, rambling lanes, gardens, foun-
tains, pavilions, and picturesque bridges. Encompassing 843 acres
enclosed by stone walls, the park is 2½ miles long (extending from
59th to 110th Streets) and a half mile wide (from Fifth Avenue to
Central Park West). It is the scene of numerous concerts, theatrical
productions, and events ranging from jogging marathons to Easter
Egg rolls. There are playing fields for numerous sports, bridal trails,

biking paths, boating lakes, a lovely zoo, gardens, and playgrounds. One could take an art tour of the dozens of statues dotting the park—many of them geared to children. And on weekends especially, musicians, acrobats, puppeteers, and other enterprising performers offer a wealth of free entertainment. Thanks to the combined efforts of the Central Park Conservancy, which, in concert with the N.Y.C. Parks Department, has spearheaded the renovation of over a third of Central Park over the last decade, the park today is safe, clean, and beautiful.

Start at the southeastern corner of the park, at:

1. **Grand Army Plaza.** The 59th Street entrance to the park is heralded by Augustus Saint-Gaudens's equestrian statue of General William T. Sherman fronted by an allegorical figure of winged victory. Its unveiling took place on Memorial Day in 1903, with bands playing *Marching Through Georgia* and a military parade (some of Sherman's men were among the marchers). Also at this corner are horse-drawn carriages. April through October, excellent trolley tours of the park depart from Fifth Avenue and 60th Street; for details and reservations (advised) call 360-2766. But that's for another time; today we walk.

Cross 60th Street and take the closest path to Fifth Avenue into the park. It leads to the:

2. **Central Park Wildlife Conservation Center (the Central Park Zoo).** Since 1864, there has been some sort of zoo in the park. Originally just a diverse collection of donated animals, the zoo became a more formal establishment in 1934 when a quadrangle of red-brick animal houses was constructed. In 1988, a renovated 5.5-acre zoo opened its doors, substituting natural-habitat enclosures for confining cages and exhibiting a cross section of international wildlife that comprises about 450 animals. Three major ecological areas are arranged around a formal English-style Central Garden that centers on a sea lion pool. The dense junglelike Tropic Zone, a rain-forest environment with streams and waterfalls, houses an aviary of brightly hued birds, along with monkeys, alligators, reptiles, and amphibians. In the Temperate Territory, Japanese snow monkeys live on an island in a lake inhabited by Arctic whooper swans; this area also has an outdoor pavilion for viewing red pandas. And the Polar Circle is home to penguins, polar bears, harbor seals, and Arctic foxes. Glass-roofed colonnaded walkways shelter zoo visitors from the elements. If you do go in, make sure to see the Intelligence Garden, with wrought-iron chairs under a rustic wooden vine-covered pagoda; it's the perfect spot for quiet contemplation.

The zoo is open 365 days a year. Admission is charged. Light fare is available at the Zoo Café.

On the Fifth Avenue side of the zoo is:

3. **The Arsenal,** a fortresslike Gothic Revival building complete with octagonal turrets. Built in the late 1840s (predating the park), it housed troops during the Civil War and was the first home of the American Museum of Natural History from 1869 to 1877. Originally, its exterior brick was covered with stucco that was later removed). Today, the brick is ivied and the Arsenal houses park headquarters, zoo administration offices, and a third-floor art gallery. Walk around to the front entrance and note the stair railing made of rifles and the weapon-related embellishments on the facade. Inside, the 1935 WPA mural by Allen Saalburg—depicting maps of New York parks, idyllic 19th-century Central Park scenes, and military themes—merits a look if you're here on a weekday when the building is open.

Up ahead is the:

4. **Delacorte Clock.** Atop an arched brick gate, this whimsical animated clock designed by Andrea Spadini has been enchanting park visitors since the mid-1960s. It features six dancing animals—a tambourine-playing bear, a kangaroo on horn, a hippo violinist, a Panlike pipe-playing goat, a penguin drummer, and an elephant squeezing an accordion. On the hour and half hour, the entire animal assemblage rotates to nursery rhyme tunes, and two bronze monkeys strike a bell. "Performances" on the hour are longer. Personally, I never tire of watching the Delacorte Clock.

To get to the next stop, you'll have to double back and make the first right after the zoo entrance where a sign indicates the way to Wollman Rink. Cross East Drive, and turn down the sloped path where you will see another sign. Cross under Gapstow Bridge on your way to:

5. **Wollman Rink.** This popular skating rink, built into the northern bay of The Pond in 1951, provides skatable ice throughout the winter season. The rest of the year it's drained and used for roller skating and rollerblading. The rink's refrigerating system broke down in 1980 and remained out of operation until real estate magnate Donald Trump came to the rescue in 1986, bringing in his own construction specialists.

En route to Wollman Rink, you'll traverse **The Pond,** originally the site of DeVoor's Mill Stream. On your left is a fenced-in bird refuge, **the Hallett Nature Sanctuary.** Where the sanctuary fence ends make a right and walk north around the rink. Make the first right, then go left to the:

6. **Chess and Checkers House.** A gift from Bernard Baruch in 1952, this octagonal hilltop facility has 10 tables indoors and 24

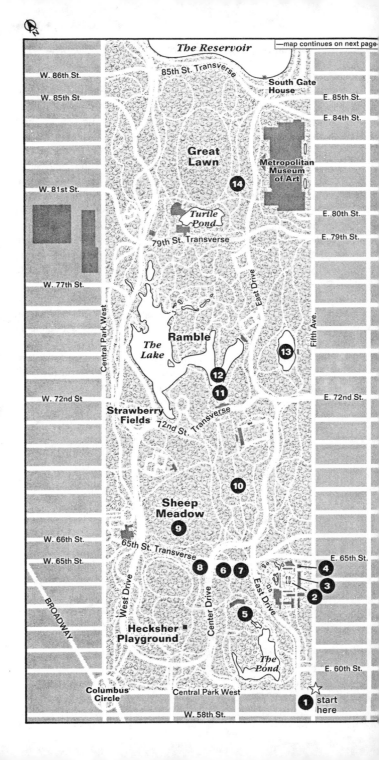

—map continues on next page

The Reservoir

W. 86th St.

W. 85th St.

85th St. Transverse

South Gate House

E. 85th St.

E. 84th St.

Great Lawn

Metropolitan Museum of Art

W. 81st St.

14

Turtle Pond

E. 80th St.

79th St. Transverse

E. 79th St.

W. 77th St.

East Drive

Ramble

The Lake

13

12

11

Central Park West

Fifth Ave.

E. 72nd St.

W. 72nd St

Strawberry Fields

72nd St. Transverse

10

Sheep Meadow

9

W. 66th St.

65th St. Transverse

W. 65th St.

E. 65th St.

8 **6** **7**

4

3

West Drive

Center Drive

East Drive

2

5

Heckscher Playground

BROADWAY

The Pond

E. 60th St.

Columbus Circle

Central Park West

W. 58th St.

1 start here

CENTRAL PARK

1. Grand Army Plaza
2. Central Park Wildlife Conservation Center
3. The Arsenal
4. Delacorte Clock
5. Wollman Rink
6. Chess and Checkers House
7. The Dairy
8. The Carousel
9. Sheep Meadow
10. The Mall
11. Bethesda Fountain
12. The Lake
13. Conservatory Water
14. The Obelisk (Cleopatra's Needle)
15. The Reservoir
16. Conservatory Garden

outside for playing these games, the latter under a circular arbor covered with vines.

Just ahead (east) is:

7. The Dairy. This Gothic Revival storybook stone cottage, designed by Vaux in 1870, was originally intended to serve fresh milk and snacks to children. Cows were stabled in a nearby building. Today, The Dairy serves as an information center, houses exhibits on the design and history of the park, offers weekend workshops (making masks, creating leaf art, or designing kites), and features free Sunday afternoon concerts in the summer. You can pick up an events calendar and informative brochures here and check out video information terminals.

Double back, going west past the Chess and Checkers House and through the tunnel (Playmates Arch) under Center Drive to:

8. The Carousel. This charming Victorian merry-go-round is one of the oldest concessions in the park. Its calliope has been playing old-fashioned tunes since 1872. The colorful whirling steeds are among the largest carousel horses in the world. Go ahead; take a ride.

Continuing west (take the path left of the carousel), you'll be walking past the Heckscher ballfields. When you come to West Drive, go north a short way (Tavern on the Green is across the street).

REFRESHMENT STOP   Tavern on the Green is located in the park at West 67th Street (tel. 873-3200). Its Victorian building was erected in 1870 to house the two hundred sheep that grazed on the Sheep Meadow; the dazzling dining room dates to 1934. Scene of numerous celebrity-studded parties, it offers patio seating under the trees in a beautiful flower garden and indoor dining, with verdant park views, in the glass-enclosed Crystal Room. The fare is American/continental, on the haute side. It's also on the pricey side but definitely worth the splurge. Open for lunch Monday to Friday from noon to 3:30pm, for brunch on Saturdays and Sundays from 10am to 3:30pm, and for dinner Sunday to Thursday from 5:30 to 11pm, Fridays and Saturdays from 5:30pm to 1am. Reservations suggested. Off-hours you can enjoy cocktails in the garden or the lounge.

Make a right on the first path you come to as you make your way north on West Drive. The path borders the:

9. Sheep Meadow. Originally a military parade ground, the Sheep Meadow entered a more peaceful incarnation in 1878.

From that year, until 1934, a flock of Southdown sheep grazed on this meadow, tended by a shepherd. Though undoubtedly picturesque, the sheep became deformed from inbreeding over the years and were banished. Today, the Sheep Meadow is a popular spot for kite flyers, sunbathers, picnickers, and Frisbee players.

Follow the fence on your right, and make a right on the gravel path of the Lilac Walk. After you pass the volleyball court area, cross the road and look for the statue of J.Q.A. Ward's *Indian Hunter*. Straight ahead (look for a group of statues) is:

10. The Mall. Designed as a Versailles-like grand promenade, this shaded formal walkway (about a quarter of a mile in length) is bordered by a double row of stately American elms that form a cathedral arch overhead. At its entrance are busts of Columbus, Shakespeare, Robert Burns, Sir Walter Scott, and American poet Fitz-Greene Halleck.

Make a right and go around the back of the bandshell through the Wisteria Pergola. At the opposite end of the mall, across 72nd Street Cross Drive, a broad stairway—its massive sandstone balustrade ornately decorated with birds, flowers, and fruit—descends to one of the park's most stunning vistas:

11. Bethesda Fountain. Emma Stebbins's biblically inspired neoclassical winged Bethesda (the "angel of the waters") tops a vast triple-tiered stone fountain with the lake forming a scenic backdrop. Its setting is Vaux's part-Gothic, part-Romanesque terrace, the heart of the park and one of its most popular venues.

Go down the steps (taking time to look closely at the bas-reliefs on the balustrades), and make a right on the path closest to:

12. The Lake. Its perimeter pathway lined with weeping willows and Japanese cherry trees, the 22 ½-acre lake was created from Sawkill Creek, which entered the Park near West 79th Street. The Neo-Victorian Loeb Boathouse at the east end of the lake rents rowboats and bicycles; in the evenings you can arrange gondola rides.

REFRESHMENT STOPS The **Boathouse Café** (tel. 517-2233), at the eastern end of the Lake, is just heavenly. Open from early spring to late November, it offers al fresco seating at lakeside tables under a white canvas canopy. Overhead heaters allow for the café's extended season. The menu is Italian/continental, featuring nouvelle pasta dishes, salads, foccacia sandwiches, and heartier entrees such as roast leg of lamb with mint butter sauce. Summer hours are Monday to Thursday from noon to 9:30pm, Fridays from noon to 11pm, Saturdays from 11:30am to 11pm, and Sundays from 11:30am to 9:30pm, with somewhat shorter hours in spring and fall. Reservations are suggested on weekends.

The Café is very elegant, but if you want something simpler—and less expensive—the Boathouse complex also houses a cafeteria with both indoor and outdoor seating. It serves full and continental breakfasts, sandwiches, chili, fresh fruit, and other light-fare items. Open year round. Hours are 9am to 6:30pm in summer, closing a little earlier the rest of the year.

From the south end of the Boathouse, cross East Drive and follow the path to the:

13. **Conservatory Water.** The above-mentioned Pond and Lake are free-form bodies of water. The Conservatory Water, scene of model boat races (there's even a model boathouse on the Fifth Avenue side where miniature craft are stored) is of formal design. Originally planned as the setting for a conservatory garden (built later and located further uptown; see Stop 16), it is the site of José de Creeft's *Alice in Wonderland* statues (Alice, the Mad Hatter, March Hare, Dormouse, and Cheshire Cat) inspired by the John Tenniel illustrations in the original 1865 edition. Overlooking the water is George Lober's Hans Christian Andersen Memorial Statue, complete with Ugly Duckling. This gift from Denmark is the setting for storytelling sessions every Saturday from June through September. Circle the pond, and peek in the model boathouse if it's open.

Exit the Conservatory Water on the northwest path (past Alice), and continue through Glade Arch, turning left after the Tranverse Road and following the path under Greywacke Arch. Bear right on the other side of the arch to:

14. **The Obelisk (Cleopatra's Needle).** This three-thousand-year-old, 77-foot-high, Egyptian pink granite obelisk was a gift to New York City from the khedive of Egypt in 1881. It was presented in thanks for America's help in building the Suez Canal. Dating from the reign of King Thothmes III, the obelisk stood in front of the Temple of the Sun in Heliopolis, Egypt, until it was removed by the Romans in 12 B.C. and placed at the approach of a temple built by Cleopatra (hence its nickname as Cleopatra's Needle). Its hieroglyphics (which are translated here, a gift of Cecil B. deMille) tell of the deeds of Thothmes III, Ramses II, and Osarkon I. The four bronze crabs peeking out from each corner of the base are 19th-century replicas of the originals, which—it is believed—were placed there by the

Romans as a decorative means of support. Crabs were objects of worship to the ancient Egyptians.

Follow the path behind the obelisk until you come to steps and a cast-iron bridge leading to the South Gate House and make a right onto the jogging path of:

15. The Reservoir, created in 1862 to supply New York City's water system. Occupying 106 acres and extending the width of the park, it is girded by bridal and jogging paths. The reservoir holds a billion gallons of water when full, is 40 feet at its greatest depth, and supplies about 10% of the city's water.

Walk—or jog—along the eastern border of the reservoir, getting off at 94th Street (a playground is directly across). Take the path paralleling the East Drive through the East Meadow, which is planted with majestic American elms and European beeches. Exit the park at 102nd Street, and walk north along Fifth Avenue to the Vanderbilt Gate. This ornate portal, designed in Paris in 1894, formerly heralded the Fifth Avenue mansion of Cornelius Vanderbilt II. Fittingly adorned with plant motifs, it is the entrance to the:

16. Conservatory Garden. This formal garden—its symmetrical paths and arbor walks contrasting with the natural look of the rest of the park—was originally the site of a complex of glass greenhouses built in 1899. They were dismantled in 1934, when Parks Commissioner Robert Moses deemed maintenance costs too high. He commissioned the current garden as a WPA project in 1936. As you enter from Fifth Avenue, you'll be facing the elegant Italian garden—a greensward with no flower beds, centering on a classic fountain. It is ringed with yew hedges and bordered by allées of crab apple trees. In spring the crab apples bloom with pink and white flowers, and narcissi grow in the ivy beneath them.

Walk through the allée on the left to the lovely mazelike English garden. It contains the bronze statue of the children from *The Secret Garden* standing in a reflecting pool (in summer there are water lilies) and a wide variety of flowering plants and shrubs—roses, butterfly bush, day lilies, clusters of blue forget-me-nots, geraniums, foxglove, and many more. Now walk through the Wisteria Pergola (at the back of the Italian garden). This flower-bedecked wrought-iron arbor, especially magnificent in late May, connects the English and French gardens.

In the French Garden, entered via rose-covered arched trellises, two levels of exquisite flower beds encircle the Untermeyer Fountain that centers on an enchanting sculpture of dancing maidens (my favorite in the park) by Walter Schott. Here, 20,000 tulips bloom in spring and 5,000 chrysanthemums in fall.

~~~~~~

The Upper West Side

~~~~~~

Start: 215 West 84th Street.
Subway: Take the 1 or 9 to 86th Street.
Finish: Lincoln Center.
Time: 3½ hours (allow more time for shopping, refreshment stops, and any museum visits).
Best Times: Weekday afternoons, when shops and museums are open but crowds are at a minimum.

The Upper West Side has undergone a decidedly upwardly mobile transformation in the last few decades. Property values have soared in response to the massive urban renewal effort that centered around the construction of Lincoln Center. Blocks of dilapidated housing and bodegas have given way to pricey boutiques and exclusive residential buildings.

Some old-timers bemoan the gentrification, but the West Side has developed an ambience all its own as the young and affluent have settled here to start families. A more democratic and informal atmosphere prevails than what you'll find on the staid and stuffy East Side. The neighborhood boasts some of the most impressive residential buildings in the city, and it's home to several world-class museums. The walking tour that follows will introduce you to the

West Side's highlights, from the architectural masterpieces on Central Park West to the heart of New York's cultural life, Lincoln Center.

Walk down Broadway from the subway station to 84th Street ("Edgar Allan Poe Street"). Just east of Broadway is:

1. **215 West 84th Street,** where a plaque commemorates the spot where Poe finished *The Raven* in 1844; he and his family once occupied a farmhouse here.

   Cross Broadway and head downtown, past one of my favorite bookstores, **Shakespeare and Company.** At the northwest corner of 80th Street stands:

2. **Zabar's,** a New York institution where you'll find throngs of shoppers clamoring for fresh crusty bread, specialty coffees, a mind-boggling selection of imported cheeses, and other gourmet delights. It's not for the faint of heart, but if you persevere and push through the crowds, you'll find the fixings for a picnic feast in Central Park or a memorable Sunday brunch.

   Don't be daunted by the long lines you are sure to see emanating from **H & H Bagels,** just across 80th Street. The bagels are so fresh that they're still warm from the oven; they're well worth the wait.

   Just south rises the magnificent limestone facade of the:

3. **Apthorp Apartments,** which command an entire square block between 78th and 79th Streets, and Broadway and West End Avenue. Admire the building from the Broadway side, standing in front of the stately iron gates, which lead into a landscaped central courtyard.

   Turn right and take 78th Street west, heading away from Broadway's bustle. Turn left down West End Avenue; at the northeast corner of 77th Street stands the Flemish-style:

4. **West End Collegiate Church and School,** accented with dormer windows and a steep red-tile roof. The church was completed in 1892 for the Collegiate Reformed Protestant Dutch Church, which was established by Dutch colonists in 1628. The Collegiate School, formed by the church in 1638, is one of the oldest independent secondary schools in the country.

   Proceed east on 77th Street back to Broadway and head downtown past **Fairway,** West Siders' favorite produce store, at 74th Street. Next, you'll see the splendid beaux arts–style:

5. **Ansonia Hotel,** between 73rd and 74th Streets, built as a luxury residence and completed in 1904. Luxurious it may be, but its architect, W. E. D. Stokes, used the roof garden to keep a small pet bear along with goats and chickens (he sold the eggs to the tenants at a discount). The Ansonia has always been a

favorite address for musicians, among them Stravinsky, Toscanini, and Caruso. (The apartments here are virtually soundproof, so musicians can practice without fear of disturbing other tenants.)

A significant bit of baseball history transpired in the Ansonia—members of the Chicago White Sox plotted to fix the World Series during a stay here in 1919. Ironically, Babe Ruth, who almost singlehandedly restored fans' faith in baseball after that disastrous scandal, moved into the Ansonia when he donned the New York Yankees' pinstripes in 1920.

Just downtown from the Ansonia is HMV, with three floors of tapes and CDs—everything from Louis Armstrong to ZZ Top. There's a remarkable selection of world beat, jazz, and progressive music, plus a well-stocked classical music annex next door.

REFRESHMENT STOP Tucked away in a basement on 72nd Street between Broadway and West End Avenue is a charming pub that hosts a crowd of neighborhood regulars. The **All State Café,** 250 West 72nd Street (tel. 874-1883), serves an impressive selection of whiskies; beer by the pitcher; and thick, juicy burgers. If you're there on a chilly winter day, you'll appreciate the fire crackling in the hearth beside the bar. Great selection of classic rock, jazz, oldies, and swing tunes on the jukebox. The All State is open daily from 11:30am to 1am (later on weekends).

Across Broadway, between 73rd and 74th Streets, is the:
6. **Apple Bank for Savings,** designed by York & Sawyer in the 1920s and boasting a massive limestone facade and stunning ironwork doors. A beautiful decorative clock, topped with twin lions, graces the downtown side of the bank. The structure was given a unique trapezoid shape to fill out the plot of land crated where Broadway cuts across Amsterdam Avenue and a heavy, monumental style that's perfectly suited to a bank building.

Take 73rd Street across to Columbus Avenue, one of New York's trendiest promenades, once full of mom-and-pop shops and now lined with upscale cafés and bars. New stores spring up like weeds on Columbus—if it's new and hip, you can find it here. Poke your head into Eurotrash (no. 301) to browse at prints and posters, or choose a vintage at Nancy's Wines (no. 313). Try Sacha of London (no. 294) and Kenneth Cole (no. 353) for up-to-the-minute styles in shoes. Putumayo (no. 341) offers affordable women's fashions with a rather bohemian, 1960s style; stop in at Goodebodies (no. 330) for an upscale selection of cosmetics and toiletries.

After you've walked a couple of blocks uptown, take a detour to the left of the avenue, to:

7. 150 West 75th Street, where Anaïs Nin lived with her mother and brother from 1914 to 1919. In the first-floor rooming house at this address, the teenaged writer began penning the diary that became her most important work.

Continue your stroll up Columbus, taking your time to allow for optimum people-watching. Make a right on 81st Street and head toward Central Park West. You'll pass a fenced-in area on the northwest lawn of the Museum of Natural History—it's a dog run, an oasis where urban canines can run free.

On your left, crowning the northwest corner of Central Park West and 81st Street is:

8. The Beresford, the first in a long line of architectural gems we'll pass on Central Park West. An adaptation of an Italian Renaissance palazzo, the Beresford, with its baroque tower and classical ornamentation, is the creation of designer Emery Roth. Gangster Meyer Lansky made his home here in the 1940s, and more recently, Rock Hudson lived here until his death from AIDS in 1985.

Make a 180° turn and you'll see the:

9. Hayden Planetarium, topped with a copper dome. (You may remember that Woody Allen fell in love with Diane Keaton while strolling through a moonscape here in *Manhattan*.) There are two floors of exhibitions on the sun, moon, and stars, and your admission includes one of the planetarium's glittering Sky Shows. The planetarium is open Monday through Friday from 12:30 to 4:45pm, Saturdays from 10am to 5:45pm, and Sundays from noon to 5:45pm; admission is charged.

Past the planetarium, turn right and start heading down Central Park West. (Turn back and look up at the Beresford after half a block or so for the best view.) Just south of the planetarium on Central Park West is the:

10. American Museum of Natural History, where an equestrian statue of Theodore Roosevelt marks the entrance. (Anthropologist Margaret Mead used to walk to her office in the museum from her home in the nearby Beresford.) The famous Hall of Dinosaurs, housing several skeletons of our predecessors, has been the highlight of many a school field trip over the years. Other highlights include an impressive collection of pre-Columbian artifacts and the largest meteorite ever retrieved.

Admission is charged, and the museum's hours are Sunday to

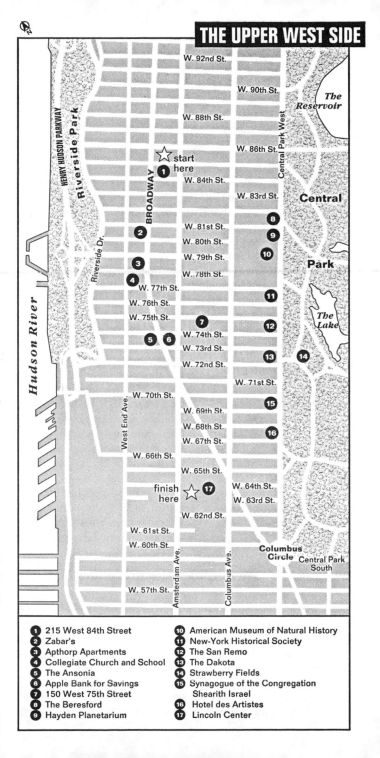

THE UPPER WEST SIDE

The Reservoir

HENRY HUDSON PARKWAY

Riverside Park

Central Park West

BROADWAY

Riverside Dr.

Central

Hudson River

Park

The Lake

West End Ave.

Amsterdam Ave.

Columbus Ave.

★ start here
① W. 84th St.
W. 92nd St.
W. 90th St.
W. 88th St.
W. 86th St.
W. 83rd St.
② W. 81st St.
⑧ W. 80th St.
⑨ W. 79th St.
③ ⑩ W. 78th St.
④ W. 77th St.
W. 76th St.
⑪ W. 75th St.
⑤ ⑥ ⑦ W. 74th St.
⑫ W. 73rd St.
⑬ W. 72nd St.
⑭ W. 71st St.
W. 70th St.
⑮ W. 69th St.
⑯ W. 68th St.
W. 67th St.
W. 66th St.
W. 65th St.
finish here ★ ⑰ W. 64th St.
W. 63rd St.
W. 62nd St.
W. 61st St.
W. 60th St.
Columbus Circle
Central Park South
W. 57th St.

❶ 215 West 84th Street	❿ American Museum of Natural History
❷ Zabar's	⓫ New-York Historical Society
❸ Apthorp Apartments	⓬ The San Remo
❹ Collegiate Church and School	⓭ The Dakota
❺ The Ansonia	⓮ Strawberry Fields
❻ Apple Bank for Savings	⓯ Synagogue of the Congregation Shearith Israel
❼ 150 West 75th Street	
❽ The Beresford	⓰ Hotel des Artistes
❾ Hayden Planetarium	⓱ Lincoln Center

Thursday from 10am to 5:45pm, and Friday and Saturday from 10am to 8:45pm.

At the southwest corner of 77th Street and Central Park West you'll see the:

11. New-York Historical Society, a rich repository of artifacts, artworks, and documents that chronicle the city's history. In addition to its renowned research library, the museum's highlights include John James Audubon's *Birds of America* watercolor series, a wonderful gallery of Tiffany lamps, and an extensive collection of early American art. The Society has recently run into funding difficulties, so if you want to go inside, you should call in advance (tel. 873-3400) to check on current hours of operation.

Once home to both Jack Dempsey and Rita Hayworth, the:

12. San Remo, 145–146 Central Park West, between 74th and 75th Streets, is another grand apartment building bearing the stamp of Emery Roth. The two towers rising at each end are crowned with columned temples.

At Central Park West and 72nd Street is a world-famous architectural masterpiece:

13. The Dakota, one of the first luxury apartment buildings in New York (so named because when the property was developed in the 1880s, it was so far north of the city center that it might as well have been in Dakota territory). Architect Henry J. Hardenbergh, who also designed New York's landmark Plaza Hotel, created a brooding, Germanic structure accented with gables, dormers, and oriel windows and surrounded by a "dry moat." (The fortresslike building was so atmospheric, in fact, that it served as the backdrop to the horror movie *Rosemary's Baby.*)

The list of tenants at this prestigious address has included Lauren Bacall, Leonard Bernstein, and Boris Karloff. But the Dakota will forever be associated with its most famous resident, John Lennon, who was gunned down just outside the building.

Lennon was returning to his home in the Dakota on December 8, 1980, when he was shot by Mark David Chapman, a lone psychopath who had asked for the former Beatle's autograph only hours earlier. Lennon's widow, Yoko Ono, still lives in the Dakota.

Just inside the 72nd Street entrance to Central Park lies:

14. Strawberry Fields, a memorial to Lennon. The three-acre teardrop-shaped "international garden of peace" is adorned with more than 150 species of plants (gifts from as many nations) and 2,500 strawberry plants. Near the entrance, a star-shaped black-and-white tile mosaic—a gift from Naples, Italy—spells out the word "Imagine." Yoko Ono provided the money for the garden's construction and maintenance.

Central Park is also a terrific vantage point from which to see the tops of the buildings you have just passed on Central Park West.

As you exit the park, you'll be right across the street from the art deco **Majestic Apartments,** another of the grand apartment houses that define the Central Park West skyline. Further down Central Park West, at the southwest corner of 70th Street, you'll see the:

15. **Synagogue of the Congregation Shearith Israel,** which dates from 1897. It's home to the oldest Jewish congregation in the United States, which was founded in 1654 by Spanish and Portuguese immigrants who came to New York via Brazil.

    Turn right on 67th Street to the:

16. **Hotel des Artistes,** whose famous residents have included Rudolph Valentino, Noël Coward, Isadora Duncan, and Norman Rockwell. The ground floor houses the elegant and romantic Café des Artistes; peek in the windows to see the famous wood-nymph murals by Howard Chandler Christy.

    Follow 67th Street to Columbus Avenue and make a left. Between 65th and 66th Streets stands the **Museum of American Folk Art** annex and its gift shop, stocked with books, jewelry, hand-painted pitchers and vases, prints, and one-of-a-kind greeting cards. Across Columbus, you can't miss:

17. **Lincoln Center,** the city's premier venue for the performing arts. In 1956, a committee headed by John D. Rockefeller III selected the site for Lincoln Center, in what was then a rundown neighborhood. *West Side Story* was filmed in these streets before an astounding 188 buildings were demolished to clear the area; 1,600 people had to be relocated to make way for the project.

    The committee commissioned a group of architects headed by Wallace K. Harrison; each building they created has classical lines, and is covered in Italian travertine. The centerpiece of the complex is an outdoor plaza graced with a café terrace and a splashing fountain. New Yorkers enjoy free entertainment under the stars here on the plaza in summer.

    Left of the plaza is Avery Fisher Hall, with a peristyle of 44 columns soaring seven stories high. It's home to the New York Philharmonic, which has counted among its musical directors such luminaries as Zubin Mehta, Arturo Toscanini, Leopold Stokowski, and Leonard Bernstein. On the right side of the fountain is the New York State Theater, designed by architect Philip Johnson, which hosts performances by the New York City Ballet and the New York City Opera.

Forming the background of the plaza is the Metropolitan Opera House, which boasts a marble colonnade 10 stories high. Inside the glass facade, you can see two large, splendid murals by Marc Chagall. The Met's interior houses seven rehearsal halls and space to store scenery for as many as 15 operas.

The remainder of the complex includes the Guggenheim Bandshell, used for free outdoor concerts; the Vivian Beaumont and Mitzi Newhouse Theaters; the world-renowned Julliard School; and Alice Tully Hall. Also at Lincoln Center is a branch of the New York Public Library, which serves as both a library and a museum of the performing arts. The library hosts an impressive array of free films and concerts, and houses an extensive collection of books on theater, music, and dance.

One-hour tours of Lincoln Center are offered for a small fee; call 875-5350 to check on the day's tour schedule and to make advance reservations.

REFRESHMENT STOP Almost any craving can be satisfied at **The Saloon,** 1920 Broadway, at 64th Street (tel. 874-1500), where the specialty is light American and continental fare—burgers, salads, individual pizzas, and much, much more. In summer the outdoor café tables are always full of avid people-watchers. You'll occasionally see the rollerskating waiters and waitresses dodging tables, diners, and the many passersby who crowd this street. The Saloon is open from 11am daily and stays open until midnight on weekdays, until 1am on weekends.

~~~~~~~

The Upper East Side

~~~~~~~

Start: 60th Street and Fifth Avenue.
Subway: Take the N or R to Fifth Avenue.
Finish: 91st Street and Fifth Avenue.
Time: Approximately 3 hours.
Best Times: Weekday afternoons, when museums and restaurants are open but not as crowded with tourists as on weekends.

Over a century ago, society watchers predicted that the wealthy and fashionable would settle permanently on the avenues bordering Central Park. Time has proven them right. Fifth Avenue north of Grand Army Plaza, which lies at the southeast corner of the park, is officially called "Museum Mile," but the magnificent private mansions built here in the first few decades of this century by some of America's wealthiest industrial tycoons also earned it the title of "Millionaires' Row." Judging from old photos, it was something to behold.

Today, some of the patrician mansions still stand along the avenue, though others have ceded their places to large apartment houses. But the age of imperial living isn't over by any means. Some of the buildings on Fifth (and on Park and elsewhere on the East Side) contain apartments that are every bit as palatial and sumptuous as the now-vanished mansions. Even New Yorkers are surprised to hear of apartments with 20, 30, or even 40 rooms—but they do exist in this neighborhood.

Start your tour on the Central Park side of Fifth Avenue, across from 60th Street. In good weather, you'll see:

1. Bookstalls lining the park. After browsing through a few old books, take a look at the view downtown—you'll see the world-famous **Plaza Hotel,** long *the* place to stay for fashionable visitors and immortalized in the children's classic *Eloise,* as the place where the heroine grew up, ordering room service nonstop and generally wreaking havoc among the staff.

Also in the immediate vicinity are several of Manhattan's classiest clubs. Just east of Fifth Avenue, at 1 East 60th Street, is the:

2. Metropolitan Club, a painted-stone Italian palace surrounded by handsome iron gates. The club was designed for J. P. Morgan by celebrated New York architects McKim, Mead, and White, who were also responsible for the building right across 60th Street, which complements the Metropolitan Club. No. 4, designed in 1905, houses the **Harmonie Club,** an elite Jewish social club.

Go back to Fifth Avenue and start heading uptown. On your right is:

3. The Pierre, one of Manhattan's priciest and most exclusive hotels since its opening in 1930. In 1932, mystery writer Dashiell Hammett stayed here while working on *The Thin Man*—though, unfortunately, he couldn't pay the bill he finally ran up. (He allegedly donned a disguise to sneak out without settling his tab.)

At the southeast corner of 62nd Street stands the third home of the:

4. Knickerbocker Club, which looks a lot like the big private houses that once characterized the avenue. The Georgian brick Knickerbocker, completed in 1915, was the work of a firm called Delano and Aldrich, a favorite of high society in the early 20th century. It retains a very pedigreed image. Ernest Hemingway, looking for peace and quiet, rented an apartment here in 1959, and stayed for about a year.

The next block up is 63rd Street and just north of it you'll see:

5. 820 Fifth Avenue, one of the earliest apartment houses built hereabouts and still one of the best. Built in 1916, it houses only one apartment on each floor, with five fireplaces and seven bathrooms in each.

Continue northward on Fifth Avenue to 64th Street. Just inside Central Park, facing 64th Street, is the:

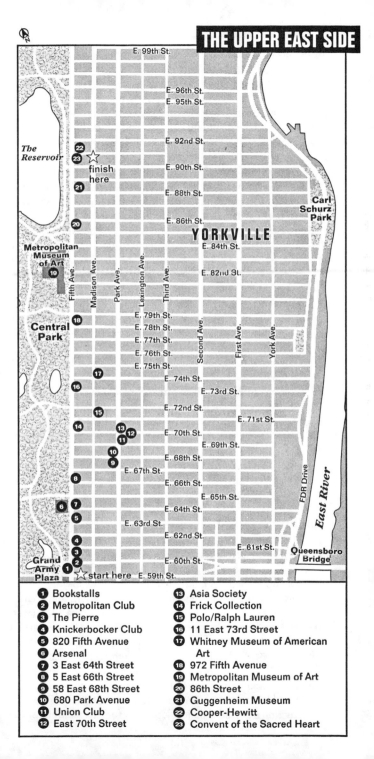

THE UPPER EAST SIDE

E. 99th St.
E. 96th St.
E. 95th St.
E. 92nd St.
E. 90th St.
E. 88th St.
E. 86th St.

YORKVILLE

E. 84th St.
E. 82nd St.

The Reservoir

finish here

Carl Schurz Park

Metropolitan Museum of Art

Central Park

E. 79th St.
E. 78th St.
E. 77th St.
E. 76th St.
E. 75th St.
E. 74th St.
E. 73rd St.
E. 72nd St.
E. 71st St.
E. 70th St.
E. 69th St.
E. 68th St.
E. 67th St.
E. 66th St.
E. 65th St.
E. 64th St.
E. 63rd St.
E. 62nd St.
E. 61st St.
E. 60th St.
start here E. 59th St.

Fifth Ave.
Madison Ave.
Park Ave.
Lexington Ave.
Third Ave.
Second Ave.
First Ave.
York Ave.

FDR Drive

East River

Grand Army Plaza

Queensboro Bridge

1. Bookstalls
2. Metropolitan Club
3. The Pierre
4. Knickerbocker Club
5. 820 Fifth Avenue
6. Arsenal
7. 3 East 64th Street
8. 5 East 66th Street
9. 58 East 68th Street
10. 680 Park Avenue
11. Union Club
12. East 70th Street
13. Asia Society
14. Frick Collection
15. Polo/Ralph Lauren
16. 11 East 73rd Street
17. Whitney Museum of American Art
18. 972 Fifth Avenue
19. Metropolitan Museum of Art
20. 86th Street
21. Guggenheim Museum
22. Cooper-Hewitt
23. Convent of the Sacred Heart

6. Arsenal, built in 1848 when this neighborhood was distant and deserted. The **Central Park Zoo** is right behind it. Across Fifth Avenue on the southeast corner of 64th Street is the former mansion of coal magnate Edward Berwind. If you've seen the mansions in Newport, Rhode Island, you've probably already seen Mr. Berwind's summer house, The Elms. His New York residence dates from 1896 and has been preserved as cooperative apartments.

Turn right (east) off Fifth Avenue onto 64th Street and proceed toward Madison Avenue. This is a particularly handsome East Side block, lined with architectural extravaganzas. Note in particular:

7. 3 East 64th Street, an opulent beaux arts mansion built in 1903 for the daughter of Mrs. William B. Astor. The house was designed by Warren and Wetmore, the firm responsible for Grand Central Terminal, and it now houses the Consulate General of India. Also worthy of admiration on this block are nos. 11, 19, and 20.

At the corner of Madison Avenue and 64th Street, turn left and proceed two blocks north to 66th Street. Madison is lined with fashionable shops and boutiques catering to the carriage trade. Note the rather fantastical apartment house built in 1900 on the northeast corner of 66th and Madison, then turn left (west) off Madison onto 66th Street, heading back toward Fifth Avenue. Among the many notable houses on this block is the magnificent French Renaissance–style house at:

8. 5 East 66th Street. It's now home to the Lotos Club, which is dedicated to literature and the fine arts, but it was built in 1900 as the city residence of William J. Schiefflin.

Next door, at 3 East 66th Street, you'll find the **home of President Ulysses S. Grant,** where he lived from 1881 to 1885. After a distastrous presidency that was marred by scandal, and after being forced to declare bankruptcy, Grant retired here to spend his last years writing his personal memoirs. Though he was battling cancer, Grant managed to hang on just long enough to complete his autobiography, which won favorable literary reviews and earned his family half a million dollars.

Now double back to Madison Avenue, turn left, and continue north for two more blocks. At 68th Street, turn right (east) toward Park Avenue. One of the best of the private houses on this block is:

9. 58 East 68th Street, on the southwest corner of the intersection with Park Avenue. Now occupied by the Council on Foreign Relations, the house was originally built in 1919 for Harold I. Pratt, son of Rockefeller partner Charles Pratt. Its construction signaled a major departure for this member of the famously close-knit Pratts. His three brothers all built mansions in Brooklyn opposite their father's. Virtually the entire family summered together in a complex of adjoining estates on Long Island. But 58 East 68th Street is in Manhattan, with no other Pratts in sight.

Walk to the north side of 68th Street to:

10. **680 Park Avenue,** a Neo-Federal town house, built in 1909 to 1911 for banker Percy Rivington Pyne and designed by McKim, Mead, and White. Its materials and scale established a character that was followed by the architects of all the subsequent houses on this Park Avenue blockfront. The building was occupied by the Soviet Mission to the United Nations from 1948 to 1963, and Soviet premier Nikita Krushchev waved to curious crowds from its Park Avenue balcony during his famous shoe-banging visit to the U.N.

    The Marquesa de Cuevas acquired the property in 1965 and saved it from the wrecker's ball by presenting it to the Americas Society, which still occupies the premises today. The society is the only national not-for-profit institution devoted to educating U.S. citizens about their Western Hemisphere neighbors. Art exhibitions and cultural programs on Latin American and Canadian affairs are open to the public.

    Go north on Park to 69th Street, then turn right and cross Park Avenue and continue eastbound on 69th Street toward Lexington Avenue. On the northeast corner of Park and 69th Street is the:

11. **Union Club,** designed in 1932 to house New York's oldest club. On the other side of 69th Street is Hunter College. Continue toward Lexington, and note 117 East 69th Street, a prototypical not-so-small private East Side house with beautiful stained-glass panels around the door.

    When you arrive at Lexington Avenue, turn left (north) and go one block uptown to 70th Street. Then turn left again (to the west) and head back toward Park Avenue along:

12. **East 70th Street,** which presents a succession of elegant houses, each more beautiful than the next. Some consider this the finest street in New York. Note in particular no. 125, a post–World War II mansion built for Paul Mellon in a French provincial style.

    When you arrive at the Park Avenue end of the block, note the modern building on the northeast corner housing the:

13. **Asia Society,** which offers changing exhibits on Asian culture and boasts an excellent gift shop and bookstore.

    Now continue across the street and note **720 Park Avenue,** on the northwest corner of the intersection. This is a prime example of the sort of swanky apartment building that lured former mansion dwellers away from their private houses. The upper floors of buildings like no. 720 often contain apartments with three or four floors and dozens of rooms.

Cross Park Avenue and continue west toward Fifth Avenue. You'll pass a lovely courtyard and pool, surrounded by stately black iron gates, before reaching the entrance to the:

14. **Frick Collection,** housed in the 1914 mansion of steel magnate Henry Clay Frick. The beautiful classic garden overlooking 70th Street was built in 1977. It definitely looks like something from the gilded age. Inside, the Frick has a notable collection of paintings—Gainsboroughs, Titians, and other treasures acquired by the Fricks over 40 years—as well as many original furnishings. Frick intended that the house, occupying a full blockfront on Fifth Avenue, be converted to a museum after his death.

The Frick Collection is open Tuesday to Saturday from 10am to 6pm, and on Sundays from 1 to 6pm (it's closed on holidays). Admission is charged; no children under 10 are admitted (children from ages 10 to 16 must be accompanied by an adult to enter).

Turn right at the corner of Fifth, passing a beautiful colonnade on the side of the Frick building. Continue two blocks north, and turn right onto 72nd Street, heading toward Madison Avenue and:

15. **Polo/Ralph Lauren.** This showcase store, housed in a renovated mansion that dates to 1895, looks for all the world like an English country place, right down to the working fireplaces, the Persian rugs, the antiques, and a grand baronial staircase. The atmosphere is that of a private men's club.

Take Madison up a block to 73rd Street; detour to your left to see:

16. **11 East 73rd Street,** a particularly sumptuous house built in 1903 by McKim, Mead, and White for Joseph Pulitzer, publisher of a once-famous but long-vanished newspaper called the *New York World.* Pulitzer rarely lived in this house because of an extreme sensitivity to sound. At one time, it contained a special soundproofed room (mounted on ball bearings, no less) to prevent vibrations. When he died in 1911, Pulitzer bequeathed $2 million to the Columbia School of Journalism, whose trustees bestow the Pulitzer prizes, annual awards for outstanding achievement in journalism, literature, drama, and musical composition.

Continue to the end of the block at Madison Avenue and turn left (north). You're now in the heart of Madison Avenue Gallery Country—stroll uptown and take time to browse in the galleries that catch your eye. You may also want to poke your head into Books and Co., a lovely bookstore on the east side of Madison, just north of 74th Street. On the southeast corner of 75th and Madison, you'll see the:

17. Whitney Museum of American Art, housed in a modern structure designed in 1966 by Marcel Breuer. The Whitney contains an impressive collection that concentrates on 20th-century American art, with paintings that reflect historical trends from naturalism to pop art and abstract expressionism. Roy Lichtenstein, Georgia O'Keeffe, Edward Hopper, and Alexander Calder are just a few of the artists represented here. Museum hours are Wednesdays and Friday through Sunday from 11am to 6pm, and Thursdays from 1 to 8pm. Admission is charged.

REFRESHMENT STOP   Inside the Whitney is a perfect place to stop for a bite—**Sarabeth's at the Whitney,** located on the lower level near the museum's sculpture garden, serves light meals and scrumptious desserts in a charming setting. Brunch is offered on weekends, and afternoon tea is served daily. Though it's housed in the museum, you don't have to pay admission charges to reach the café.

Continue uptown on Madison. At 76th Street, you'll pass one of New York's grand old hotels, **the Carlyle,** which has counted two presidents among its famous guests—Harry Truman and John Kennedy. Turn left (west) when you reach 79th Street and return to Fifth Avenue. There's an impressive row of buildings here—everything from French château–style structures to neo-Georgian town houses. When you reach the corner of Fifth, turn left for a look at:

18. 972 Fifth Avenue, which lies between 78th and 79th Streets. It is now the French Embassy's Cultural Services Office, but it was built in 1906 as a wedding present for one Payne Whitney by his doting (and childless) rich uncle. This McKim, Mead, and White opus cost $1 million and was the talk of the town in its day.

Next door, on the corner of 78th Street, is the classic French-style mansion of tobacco millionaire James B. Duke (as in Duke University). His daughter Doris occupied the house intermittently until 1957, when she donated it to New York University. NYU now operates it as a fine arts institute.

Now turn around and walk north on Fifth Avenue until you reach 82nd Street. On your left is the grand entrance of the:

19. Metropolitan Museum of Art, one of New York's greatest cultural institutions. The block of 82nd Street that faces the museum's mammoth staircase almost acts as a sort of formal court.

The Met's collection is the largest in the Western Hemisphere, ranging from a world-class Egyptian collection that boasts tens of thousands of objects to a popular gallery that displays a dazzling array of impressionist and post-impressionist paintings.

Museum hours are Sundays and Tuesday through Thursday from 9:30am to 5:15pm, Fridays and Saturdays from 9:30am to 8:45pm. There's a suggested contribution if you decide to enter and browse for awhile; however, it would take weeks to see all of the Met's treasures, so it might be best to save it for another day and merely admire the exterior for now.

Continue uptown to:

20. 86th Street. The big brick-and-limestone mansion on the southeastern corner of Fifth Avenue and 86th Street was built in 1914 for William Star Miller. It was to this house Mrs. Cornelius Vanderbilt retreated in 1944 when her famous 640 Fifth Avenue house was sold. No. 640 Fifth Avenue was located down on 51st Street; by 1944, Mrs. V. was pretty much alone down there, surrounded by ghosts of the Vanderbilt past and lots of noisy traffic and new office buildings. No. 640 Fifth Avenue was the first of a concentration of Vanderbilt family houses that at one time caused Fifth Avenue in the 1950s to be called "Vanderbilt Alley." The exile to 86th Street appears, at least from the look of this house, to have been comfortable, anyway.

Two blocks further up Fifth Avenue is the:

21. Guggenheim Museum, between 88th and 89th Streets, whose building piques just as much interest as the collection of modern masterpieces it houses. Designed by Frank Lloyd Wright in 1959, it set off a storm of architectural controversy when it was built. Nowadays, New Yorkers have grown to think of the building as a treasured landmark—so much so that the recent addition of new exhibition space sparked an outcry among those who felt that the city's only building designed by Wright should never be altered. The structure has a unique spiral shape; visitors generally take an elevator to the top floor, then walk down the ramp, viewing the artworks hung along the curved walls.

The Guggenheim's hours are Friday through Wednesday from 10am to 8pm. Admission is charged.

Uptown from the Guggenheim is another major museum, the:

22. Cooper-Hewitt, housed in the former Andrew Carnegie mansion. Built in 1901, this Georgianesque palace originally shared the neighborhood with squatters' shanties and roaming pigs. By the time the squatters were gone and the streets were built up with fine houses, Carnegie was dead. His widow lived on in the house until 1949.

Across 91st Street from the Cooper-Hewitt is the:

23. Convent of the Sacred Heart, occupying what was once the largest private house ever built in Manhattan. Constructed for financier Otto Kahn, it survives in pretty much its original condition. Other houses on this 91st Street block, notably nos. 7 and 9, are almost as grand.

Take 91st Street east to Madison Avenue and turn right (downtown) if you'd like to end our tour with a pick-me-up.

REFRESHMENT STOP   A lovely tea room and pastry shop, **Les Delices Guy Pascal,** 1231 Madison Avenue, at 89th Street (tel. 289-5300), is surprisingly inexpensive for pricey Madison Avenue. It's open and airy, with small pots of flowers atop cool blue floral-print tablecloths. The desserts are enticing, and might go well with a cup of cappuccino. The sandwiches and fresh salads are complemented by a selection of more substantial French and continental dishes, including a changing list of daily specials, most under $10.

~~~~~~~

Brooklyn Heights

~~~~~~~

Start: Borough Hall.
Subway: Take the N, R, 2, or 3 to Borough Hall.
Finish: Montague Terrace.
Time: Approximately 3 hours.
Best Times: Weekends.

Brooklyn Heights, with its gracious brownstones and tree-lined streets, is all too often overlooked by tourists in their mad rush to see the sights of Manhattan. Some misguided souls might even think that the only thing to see out here is the view of the Manhattan skyline across the river. They're in for a pleasant surprise, since the neighborhood is dotted with historic sites and magnificent buildings.

When Robert Fulton's ferry began making the run to and from Manhattan, it brought with it a wave of city dwellers eager to purchase suburban homes. Brooklyn Heights had, up until this point, been a rural farming village, but the influx of new residents, most of them upper-middle-class Protestants, changed its character forever.

Brooklyn Heights rose to prominence and prosperity in the 19th century, becoming much more than a mere bedroom community for Manhattan. Prior to the Civil War, it became a leading center for the abolitionist movement. In those years, the neighborhood was home to Walt Whitman and Henry Ward Beecher, both of whom profoundly influenced American thought in the mid-1800s. As you stroll along the route laid out below, you'll see that Brooklyn Heights has never ceased to attract writers and intellectuals.

Start at the south end of Cadman Plaza, at Court and Remsen Streets, where:

1. **Borough Hall** sits crowned with an impressive cupola. This imposing structure was completed in 1849, just as New York City's shipping industry began to boom with the opening of the Erie Canal and Brooklyn was transformed from a farming village into a major center for commerce. Borough Hall was a tremendous source of pride for the neighborhood, and it served as Brooklyn's City Hall until 1898, when Brooklyn was incorporated into the City of New York.

Now take Court Street south for several blocks and make a right turn onto:

2. **Atlantic Avenue,** the center of New York's Arab community. In the 1940s, construction on the new Brooklyn Battery Tunnel demolished much of Manhattan's Arab neighborhood, and many of its residents headed for new quarters along Atlantic Avenue. Today, this area is home to Syrians, Lebanese, Palestinians, and Yemenis, and it's lined with Arab coffeehouses, bakeries, and emporiums.

The Damascus Bakery, at 195 Atlantic Avenue, is the place to buy Syrian flatbreads and date cakes. Take a peek inside the Sahadi Importing Company, at no. 187, for a mind-boggling selection of merchandise that runs the gamut from spices and teas to crafts and fabrics. At no. 170 is the Oriental Pastry and Grocery, where you can purchase freshly baked pastries or all the ingredients to whip up your own sugary concoctions.

REFRESHMENT STOP If the exotic sights and smells of Atlantic Avenue have given you hunger pangs, head for **Tripoli,** at no. 156 (tel. 718/596-5800), an authentic Lebanese restaurant adorned with brightly painted murals. Try the Tripoli Maza, a generous sampler plate of hummus, baba ghanoush, felafel, and salad; perhaps you'll be tempted by the subtly flavored suumuk b'tahini, a fish filet sautéed in spicy tahini sauce with walnuts and almonds. You can have a satisfying meal here for less than $10. Tripoli is open daily from 11am to 11pm.

From Atlantic Avenue, turn right on Henry Street and then take a left onto State Street. The very next right turn will bring you to:

3. **Garden Place,** a lovely block lined with carriage houses and

charming residences. The locals sometimes refer to this affluent area as the "Scarsdale of Brooklyn Heights."

Garden Place ends at Joralemon Street, where you'll turn left before making a right onto Hicks Street. (Hicks Street, by the way, was named after a prominent local farming family—from whose name snobbish city dwellers coined the term "hick" to refer to country and farm folk.) Take the first street branching off to your left, a tranquil little cul-de-sac called:

4. Grace Court. At the corner stands Grace Episcopal Church, a Gothic Revival sandstone structure designed in 1847 by Richard Upjohn; it boasts three stained-glass windows by Louis Comfort Tiffany. Arthur Miller owned no. 31 from 1947 to 1951, and it was here that he penned his most famous work, *Death of a Salesman.* If you walk to the end of Grace Court, you'll get a glimpse of the East River and the Manhattan skyline.

Retrace your steps back to Hicks Street and continue north for another block. Now make a right onto Remsen Street. At the corner of Henry Street stands the:

5. Our Lady of Lebanon Cathedral, also designed by Upjohn. This church, however, was acquired by the Maronite Christians of the Lebanese community in 1944, who incorporated Middle Eastern design touches into the structure. Notice the Mediterranean-themed mural over the altar, the Arabic-style calligraphic designs that border the walls and ceilings, and the stained-glass windows that are reminiscent of mosaic patterns. Take a minute to admire the intricate panels at the southern and western portals—they were rescued from the *Normandie,* an ocean liner that burned in 1942.

Take Henry Street north two blocks to Pierrepont Street. At the southwest corner is the:

6. Herman Behr House, a magnificent residential building designed by Frank Freeman in the Romanesque Revival style. The original structure was enlarged to become the Hotel Palm, before it was reincarnated as a brothel (the roster of tenants underwent a dramatic change when the building was later acquired by the Catholic church). It was eventually sold for conversion to co-op apartments in 1976.

Now look for:

7. 102 Pierrepont Street, where Arthur Miller lived for three years and where he penned *All My Sons.* Another literary giant, Norman Mailer, lived upstairs with his parents; it was here that he wrote *The Naked and the Dead.*

Continue east along Pierrepont Street, admiring the handsome brownstones. On your left, at the corner of Monroe Place, stands the Gothic-style sandstone:

8. **First Unitarian Church,** the oldest church building in Brooklyn Heights (it was consecrated in 1844). It was commissioned by a group of Unitarian merchants who were ostracized by their more conservative Protestant counterparts in New England and came to settle in New York. The church is graced with a series of glass windows designed by Louis Comfort Tiffany.

Continue east on Pierrepont Street toward Clinton Street until you reach the massive red-brick Romanesque building that houses the:

9. **Brooklyn Historical Society** (formerly the Long Island Historical Society but renamed under pressure from neighborhood residents). The prints and artifacts in the gallery celebrate Brooklyn's history and heritage, from the still-beloved Brooklyn Dodgers to Coney Island. Upstairs is a reading room crammed with a vast collection of maps, photographs, newspapers, and manuscripts. The gallery is open Wednesday through Saturday from noon to 5pm; the library's hours are Tuesday through Saturday from 10am to 4:45pm. Admission is charged.

Notice the magnificent Italian palatial–style bank building just across Clinton Street—it's a branch of Manufacturers Hanover, designed by York & Sawyer, the same architects responsible for the Federal Reserve Bank and the Apple Bank for Savings in Manhattan.

Now take Clinton Street one block south; at the northwest corner of Clinton and Montague Streets stands the:

10. **Church of St. Ann and the Holy Trinity,** built in 1843 to 1847. Don't miss the chance to see the church's stained-glass windows, created by William Bolton; they're among the first made in the United States. St. Ann's has long been one of the most prestigious congregations among the upper middle class of Brooklyn Heights.

Now stroll east on Montague Street for a block and turn left on Court Street, heading north. Soon you'll reach:

11. **Cadman Plaza,** which was created by an urban renewal project in the 1950s. Stroll north through the plaza and park, toward the Brooklyn Bridge. You'll come upon a statue of Robert F. Kennedy, who was New York's senator during his 1968 presidential bid; he was assassinated after a campaign appearance in Los Angeles. Also in Cadman Plaza is a grand U.S. Post Office building, an impressive example of Romanesque Revival architecture. As you keep going, you'll pass memorials to the Brooklyn servicemen and servicewomen who died in World War II.

When you exit the plaza near the north end, you'll find yourself on Cadman Plaza West. A few blocks north of our route, near Old Fulton Street, once stood a print shop, long since

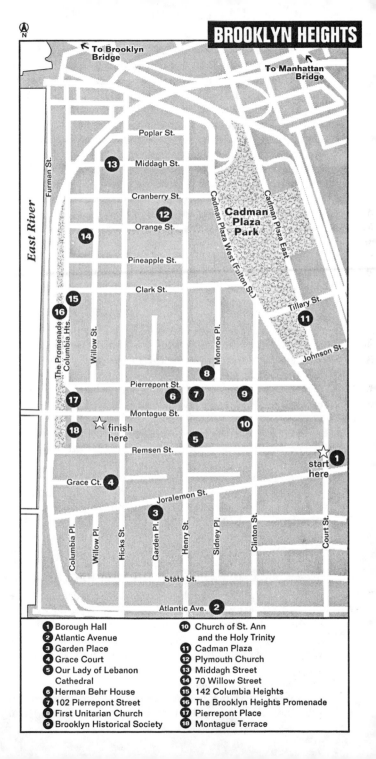

BROOKLYN HEIGHTS

N

To Brooklyn Bridge

To Manhattan Bridge

East River

Furman St.

Poplar St.

Middagh St. **13**

Cranberry St.

Orange St. **12**

14

Pineapple St.

Clark St.

15

16

The Promenade
Columbia Hts.

Willow St.

Monroe Pl.

8

Pierrepont St. **6** **7** **9**

17

Montague St. **10**

5

Remsen St.

★ finish here

18

★ start here **1**

Cadman Plaza Park

Cadman Plaza West (Fulton St.)

Cadman Plaza East

Tillary St.

11

Johnson St.

Grace Ct. **4**

Joralemon St.

3

Columbia Pl.

Willow Pl.

Hicks St.

Garden Pl.

Henry St.

Sidney Pl.

Clinton St.

Court St.

State St.

Atlantic Ave. **2**

1 Borough Hall
2 Atlantic Avenue
3 Garden Place
4 Grace Court
5 Our Lady of Lebanon
   Cathedral
6 Herman Behr House
7 102 Pierrepont Street
8 First Unitarian Church
9 Brooklyn Historical Society

10 Church of St. Ann
   and the Holy Trinity
11 Cadman Plaza
12 Plymouth Church
13 Middagh Street
14 70 Willow Street
15 142 Columbia Heights
16 The Brooklyn Heights Promenade
17 Pierrepont Place
18 Montague Terrace

demolished, where Walt Whitman reportedly set the type for his most important collection of poetry, *Leaves of Grass*. (Whitman lived in Brooklyn for many years, and served as editor-in-chief of the *Brooklyn Eagle*. Like many neighborhood residents, he was an ardent abolitionist—during the Civil War he worked tending the wounded, and his poem *O Captain, My Captain* was written as a tribute to Lincoln.) An apartment building now stands here, however, and no plaque marks the site, so you may want to continue on to the next stop.

From Cadman Plaza West, walk one block on Cranberry Street and make a left onto Henry Street; now turn right on Orange Street. Here stands the Congregationalist:

12. **Plymouth Church of the Pilgrims,** whose exterior appearance is reminiscent of a New England meeting house. The statue in the courtyard beside the church is of Henry Ward Beecher, pastor of the church for more than 40 years in the mid-19th century. One of the most influential figures in Brooklyn Heights' history, Beecher was a leading abolitionist, as was his sister, Harriet Beecher Stowe, who authored *Uncle Tom's Cabin*. Beside Beecher's figure you'll see another statue, this one of a slave girl named Pinky. Beecher auctioned her off to his congregation in 1854 to dramatize the horrors of slavery (the parishioners got the point—they bought her freedom). Plymouth Church was a stop on the Underground Railroad, a network of abolitionists who aided and housed slaves escaping to the North.

Inside the church before you, Beecher delivered his fiery, eloquent sermons denouncing slavery. He traveled to England on a speaking tour that was so successful he was credited with turning British public opinion against the South. When the Civil War ended and the Union was restored, Abraham Lincoln asked Beecher to deliver the invocation at the flag-raising ceremony at Fort Sumter.

Beecher met his match when he tangled with journalist Victoria Woodhull, however, and one of the juiciest scandals of the late 19th century ensued. Beecher, at the peak of his influence after the war, was the highest-paid preacher in the nation when Woodhull took him to task for condemning "free love" in public—while in private he was carrying on an affair with one of his parishioners, a married woman named Elizabeth Tilton. Her husband sued Beecher for alienation of his wife's affection, and though Beecher was never held liable in court, his straight-laced congregation, made up of Brooklyn's conservative middle class, was thoroughly shocked.

Though the church will be forever associated with Beecher, other notables who spoke here include Clara Barton, John

Greenleaf Whittier, Ralph Waldo Emerson, Booker T. Washington, Charles Dickens, and Mark Twain. Abraham Lincoln once worshipped here as well, and the church also holds a fragment of Plymouth Rock.

Now turn right onto Hicks Street and head north, past Cranberry Street, admiring the handsome brownstones that you pass. Turn left onto:

13. **Middagh Street.** The house that once stood at no. 7 was demolished to accommodate expressway traffic—a tragedy for literary enthusiasts. Carson McCullers, W. H. Auden, and George Davis, the literary editor of *Harper's Bazaar,* set up housekeeping at this address in the early 1940s. (The house's cook was referred to the trio by famed stripper Gypsy Rose Lee.) An amazing roster of literary types and other celebrities passed through these doors. Jane and Paul Bowles rented a floor here, and Anaïs Nin, Salvador Dalí, and Aaron Copland visited at one time or another. Richard Wright took the basement apartment with his wife and child, but only briefly; he found the house's atmosphere too chaotic, "not a proper environment in which to raise a child."

Take Middagh Street to Willow Street and turn left. Between Pineapple and Orange Streets, you'll come to a magnificent house at:

14. **70 Willow Street.** Truman Capote wrote *In Cold Blood* and *Breakfast at Tiffany's* while he was a tenant in the basement apartment.

Retrace your steps back to Orange Street; take Orange one block west and turn left onto Columbia Heights. The building that once stood at no. 110 was once home to both Hart Crane and John Dos Passos in the 1920s. Washington Roebling, who masterminded the Brooklyn Bridge's construction, was confined to his bed here after overseeing the project ruined his health. (He insisted on diving into the East River with the workmen as the pilings were put in place, and he, like many of the construction workers, fell victim to the bends.)

Head south and look for:

15. **142 Columbia Heights,** where author Norman Mailer has lived for many years.

Now, near Clark Street, take the path on your right that leads to the:

16. **Brooklyn Heights Promenade** (also referred to as the Esplanade). Stretching before you is a breathtaking view of the Manhattan skyline, dominated by the twin towers of the World Trade Center. If you can pry your gaze away from the sight of Manhattan's skyscrapers, you'll see the Statue of Liberty holding her torch over the harbor. Nearby lies Ellis Island—12 million

people from every corner of the world passed through the doors of the immigration facility here, hoping to begin a better life in America.

Wander south and take in the view at your leisure; if you're here on a pleasant summer afternoon, the promenade will be lined with artists and vendors, making for a wonderful stroll.

Leave the promenade near the south end at:

17. Pierrepont Place. At no. 3 stands the A. A. Low House, a brownstone that was home to one of the most influential and prosperous figures in New York's 19th-century shipping industry and China trade. (A. A. Low's son Seth went on to become mayor of New York in the early 1900s.)

Near the brownstone at 2 Pierrepont Place you'll see a plaque where the Four Chimneys once stood; George Washington stayed here during the Battle of Long Island. (Washington almost lost the entire Continental Army in Brooklyn in 1776 by neglecting to block off a small road near Flatbush. The British troops surrounded the rebellious colonists, and only a blanket of fog allowed Washington and his troops to escape to Manhattan.)

Just below Pierrepont Place, across Montague Street, is:

18. Montague Terrace, boasting a row of town houses built in the 1880s. W. H. Auden occupied no. 1, and in the early 1930s, Thomas Wolfe completed work on *Of Time and the River* while living at no. 5.

Now you can finish off your tour by wandering east along Montague Street, which may remind Bostonians of Newberry Street. Browse in the shops or stop in one of the many cafés you'll pass on your way back to the subway at Borough Hall.

REFRESHMENT STOP Montague Street is the heart of Brooklyn Heights, and it offers numerous spots to stop for a bite, whether you're craving sushi, enchiladas, or sweet-and-sour shrimp. A longtime favorite in the neighborhood is the **Montague Street Saloon,** an informal pub-style spot where you can enjoy inexpensive burgers, salads, omelets, and sandwiches. (Don't miss the French onion soup.)

APPENDIX

Recommended Reading

GENERAL

Alleman, Richard, *The Movie Lover's Guide to New York* (Harper & Row, 1988).

Bayles, W. H., *Old Taverns of New York* (Gordon Press, 1977).

Black, Mary, *Old New York in Early Photographs: Eighteen Fifty-Three to Nineteen Hundred & One* (Dover, 1973).

Cohen, Barbara, et al, eds., *New York Observed: Artists & Writers Look at the City, 1650 to the Present* (Abrams, 1987).

Cudahy, Brian J., *Over and Back* (Fordham University Press, 1989).

Delaney, Edmund T., and Lockwood, Charles, *Greenwich Village: A Photographic Guide* (Dover, 1984).

Dolkart, Andrew S., *The Texture of TriBeCa* (TriBeCa Community Association, 1989).

Dunlap, David W., *On Broadway* (Rizzoli International, 1990).

Edmiston, Susan, and Cirino, Linda, *Literary New York* (Houghton Mifflin, 1976).

Fine, Jo R. and Wolfe, Gerard R., *The Synagogues of the Lower East Side* (New York University Press, 1978).

Furia, Philip, *The Poets of Tin Pan Alley* (Oxford University Press, 1990).

Gody, Lou, *The WPA Guide to New York City* (Pantheon, 1982).

Kieran, John, *A Natural History of New York City* (Fordham, 1982).

Kinkead, Eugene, *Central Park: The Birth, Decline, and Renewal of a National Treasure* (Norton, 1990).

Kisseloff, Jeff, *You Must Remember This* (Schocken Books, 1989).

Leisner, Marcia, *Literary Neighborhoods of New York* (Starrhill Press, 1989).

Marquesee, Mike and Harris, Bill, eds., *New York: An Anthology* (Cadogan Publications, 1985).

McDarrah, Fred, *Greenwich Village* (Citadel Press, 1963).

Miller, Terry, *Greenwich Village and How It Got That Way* (Crown Publishers, 1990).

Moorhouse, Geoffrey, *Imperial City: New York* (H. Holt & Co., 1988).

Morris, Jan, *Manhattan '45* (Oxford University Press, 1987).

Plumb, Stephen, *The Streets Where They Lived* (MarLor Press, 1989).

Schermerhorn, Gene, *Letters to Phil* (New York Bound, 1982).

Shepard, Richard F., *Broadway from the Battery to the Bronx* (Harry N. Abrams, 1988).

Simon, Kate, *New York Places and Pleasures* (Meridien Books, 1959).

Snyder, Robert, *The Voice of the City: Vaudeville and Popular Culture in New York* (Oxford University Press, 1989).

Trager, James, *Park Avenue: Street of Dreams* (Atheneum Publishers, 1989).

Trager, James, *West of Fifth: The Rise and Fall of Manhattan's West Side* (Atheneum Publishers, 1987).

ECONOMIC, POLITICAL & SOCIAL HISTORY

Abbott, Berenice, *New York in the Thirties* (Dover, 1973).

Allen, Oliver E., *New York, New York: A History of the World's Most Exhilarating & Challenging City* (Macmillan, 1990).

Asbury, Herbert, *The Gangs of New York* (Capricorn Books, 1989).

Baldwin, James, *Notes of a Native Son* (Beacon Press, 1990).

Blackmar, Elizabeth, *Manhattan for Rent, Seventeen Eighty-five to Eighteen Fifty* (Cornell University Press, 1988).

Bender, Thomas, *New York Intellect: A History of Intellectual Life in New York City from 1750 to the Beginnings of Our Own Time* (University of Illinois Press, 1988).

Brandt, Nat, *The Man Who Tried to Burn New York* (Syracuse University Press, 1986).

Cohen, B., Heller, S., and Chwast, S., *New York Observed* (Harry N. Abrams, 1987).

Ellis, Edward Robb, *The Epic of New York City: A Narrative History* (Old Town Books, 1966).

Feninger, Andreas, *New York in the Forties* (Dover, 1978).

Gambee, Robert, *Wall Street Christmas* (Norton, 1990).

Jacobs, William Jay, *Ellis Island* (Macmillan, 1990).

Kazin, Alfred, *Our New York* (Harper & Row Publishers, 1989).

Kessner, Thomas, *Fiorello H. La Guardia and the Making of Modern New York* (McGraw-Hill Publishing Co., 1989).

Kinkead, Gwen, *Chinatown: A Portrait of a Closed Society* (HarperCollins, 1992).

Koch, Edward, *Mayor: An Autobiography* (Simon & Schuster, 1984) and *Politics* (Simon & Schuster, 1986).

Kotker, Norman, *Ellis Island* (Macmillan, 1990).

Leeds, Mark, *Ethnic New York* (Passport Books, 1991).

MacKay, Ernst A., *The Civil War & New York City* (Syracuse University Press, 1990).

McCullough, David, *The Great Bridge* (Simon & Schuster, 1983).

Mitchell, Joseph, *Up in the Old Hotel* (Pantheon, 1992).

Morris, Lloyd, *Incredible New York: High Life & Low Life of the Last Hundred Years* (Ayer Co. Publishers, 1975).

Patterson, Jerry E., *The Vanderbilts* (Harry N. Abrams, 1989).

Plunz, Richard A., *A History of Housing in New York City* (Columbia University Press, 1990).

Rink, Oliver A., *Holland on the Hudson* (New York State Historical Association, 1986).

Sanders, Ronald, *The Downtown Jews: Portraits of an Immigrant Generation* (Harper & Row, 1969).

Sante, Luc, *Low Life: Lures and Snares of Old New York* (Farrar, Straus, Giroux, 1991).

White, E. B., *Here Is New York* (Warner Books, 1988).

ARCHITECTURE & THE ARTS

Bogart, Michele H., *Public Sculpture and the Civic Ideal in New York City 1890–1989* (University of Chicago Press, 1989).

Boyer, M. Christine, *Manhattan Manners: Architecture & Style 1850–1900* (Rizzoli International, 1985).

Dolkart, Andrew S., *Guide to New York City Landmarks* (Preservation Press, 1992).

Gayle, Margot and Cohen, Michele, *Manhattan's Outdoor Sculpture* (Prentice Hall Press, 1988).

Gayle, Margot and Gillon, Edmund V., *Cast-Iron Architecture in New York* (Dover, 1974).

Goldberger, Paul, *The City Observed—New York: A Guide to*

the Architecture of Manhattan (Vintage Books, 1979) and *Skyscraper* (Knopf, 1983).

Harrison, Marina and Rosenfeld, Lucy D., *Artwalks in New York* (Michael Kesend Publishing, 1991).

Lieberman, Nathaniel, *Manhattan Lightscape* (Abbeville Press, 1990).

Mackay, Donald A., *The Building of Manhattan: How Manhattan Was Built Overground & Underground, from the Dutch Settlers to the Skyscrapers* (Harper & Row Publishers, 1987).

Marshall, Richard, *Fifty New York Artists: A Critical Selection of Painters & Sculptors Working in New York* (Chronicle Books, 1986).

Orkin, Ruth, *More Pictures from My Window* (Rizzoli International, 1985).

Rajs, Jake, *Manhattan: An Island in Focus* (Rizzoli International, 1985).

Reed, Henry Hope and Sophia Duckworth, *Central Park: A History and a Guide* (Clarkson N. Potter, Inc., 1972).

Rosen, Laura, *Top of the City: New York's Hidden Rooftop World* (Thames & Hudson, 1990).

Silver, Nathan, *Lost New York* (American Legacy, 1982).

Stern, Robert A. M., Gilmartin, Gregory, and Massengale, John M., *New York 1900: Metropolitan Architecture and Urbanism 1890–1915* (Rizzoli International, 1983).

Valenzi, Kathleen D., ed., *Private Moments: Images of Manhattan* (Howell Press, 1989).

von Pressentinwright, Carol, *Blue Guide New York* (W. W. Norton & Co., 1991).

Watson, Edward B., *New York Then & Now: Eighty-three Manhattan Sites Photographed in the Past & Present* (Dover Publications, 1976).

Willensky, Elliot, and White, Norval, *AIA Guide to New York City* (Harcourt Brace Jovanovich, 1989).

FICTION FOR ADULTS

Cooper, James F., *The Last of the Mohicans* (State University of New York Press, 1983).

Finney, Jack, *Time and Again* (Simon & Schuster, 1986).

Fitzgerald, F. Scott, *The Great Gatsby* (Macmillan, 1981).

James, Henry, *Washington Square* (G. K. Hall & Co., 1980).

Janowitz, Tama, *Slaves of New York* (Crown, 1986).

Liebling, A. J., *The Telephone Booth Indian* (North Point Press, 1990).

McInerney, Jay, *Bright Lights, Big City* (Random House, 1984).

Powell, Dawn, *The Locusts Have No King* (Yarrow Press, 1989).

Wharton, Edith, *The Age of Innocence* (Macmillan, 1983).

FICTION FOR KIDS

Barracca, Sal, *The Adventures of Taxi Dog* (Halcyon Books, 1990).

Gangloff, Deborah, *Albert and Victoria* (Crown Publishers, 1989).

Macaulay, David, *Underground* (Houghton Mifflin Co., 1976).

Selden, George, *The Cricket in Times Square* (Dell Publishing Co., 1970).

Swift, Hildegarde H., *The Little Red Lighthouse and the Great Gray Bridge* (Harcourt Brace Jovanovich, 1974).

Thomson, Kay, *Eloise* (Simon & Schuster, 1969).

Waber, Bernard, *Lyle, Lyle, Crocodile and the House on East 88th Street* (Houghton Mifflin Co., 1965).

White, E. B., *Stuart Little* (Harper & Row Publishers, 1973).

Index

Please Send Me the Books Checked Below.
FROMMER'S COMPREHENSIVE GUIDES
(Guides listing facilities from budget to deluxe,
with emphasis on the medium-priced)

	Retail Price	Code		Retail Price	Code
☐ Acapulco/Ixtapa/Taxco 1993–94	$15.00	C120	☐ Jamaica/Barbados 1993–94	$15.00	C105
☐ Alaska 1990–91	$15.00	C001	☐ Japan 1992–93	$19.00	C020
☐ Arizona 1993–94	$18.00	C101	☐ Morocco 1992–93	$18.00	C021
☐ Australia 1992–93	$18.00	C002	☐ Nepal 1992–93	$18.00	C038
☐ Austria 1993–94	$19.00	C119	☐ New England 1993	$17.00	C114
☐ Austria/Hungary 1991–92	$15.00	C003	☐ New Mexico 1993–94	$15.00	C117
☐ Belgium/Holland/ Luxembourg 1993–94	$18.00	C106	☐ New York State 1992–93	$19.00	C025
☐ Bermuda/Bahamas 1992–93	$17.00	C005	☐ Northwest 1991–92	$17.00	C026
☐ Brazil 1993–94	$20.00	C111	☐ Portugal 1992–93	$16.00	C027
☐ California 1993	$18.00	C112	☐ Puerto Rico 1993–94	$15.00	C103
☐ Canada 1992–93	$18.00	C009	☐ Puerto Vallarta/ Manzanillo/Guadalajara 1992–93	$14.00	C028
☐ Caribbean 1993	$18.00	C102	☐ Scandinavia 1993–94	$19.00	C118
☐ Carolinas/Georgia 1992–93	$17.00	C034	☐ Scotland 1992–93	$16.00	C040
☐ Colorado 1993–94	$16.00	C100	☐ Skiing Europe 1989–90	$15.00	C030
☐ Cruises 1993–94	$19.00	C107	☐ South Pacific 1992–93	$20.00	C031
☐ DE/MD/PA & NJ Shore 1992–93	$19.00	C012	☐ Spain 1993–94	$19.00	C115
☐ Egypt 1990–91	$15.00	C013	☐ Switzerland/Liechtenstein 1992–93	$19.00	C032
☐ England 1993	$18.00	C109	☐ Thailand 1992–93	$20.00	C033
☐ Florida 1993	$18.00	C104	☐ U.S.A. 1993–94	$19.00	C116
☐ France 1992–93	$20.00	C017	☐ Virgin Islands 1992–93	$13.00	C036
☐ Germany 1993	$19.00	C108	☐ Virginia 1992–93	$14.00	C037
☐ Italy 1993	$19.00	C113	☐ Yucatan 1993–94	$18.00	C110

FROMMER'S $-A-DAY GUIDES
(Guides to low-cost tourist accommodations and facilities)

	Retail Price	Code		Retail Price	Code
☐ Australia on $45 1993–94	$18.00	D102	☐ Israel on $45 1993–94	$18.00	D101
☐ Costa Rica/Guatemala/ Belize on $35 1993–94	$17.00	D108	☐ Mexico on $50 1993	$19.00	D105
☐ Eastern Europe on $30 1993–94	$18.00	D110	☐ New York on $70 1992–93	$16.00	D016
☐ England on $60 1993	$18.00	D107	☐ New Zealand on $45 1993–94	$18.00	D103
☐ Europe on $45 1993	$19.00	D106	☐ Scotland/Wales on $50 1992–93	$18.00	D019
☐ Greece on $45 1993–94	$19.00	D100	☐ South America on $40 1993–94	$19.00	D109
☐ Hawaii on $75 1993	$19.00	D104	☐ Turkey on $40 1992–93	$22.00	D023
☐ India on $40 1992–93	$20.00	D010	☐ Washington, D.C. on $40 1992	$17.00	D024
☐ Ireland on $40 1992–93	$17.00	D011			

FROMMER'S CITY $-A-DAY GUIDES
(Pocket-size guides with an emphasis on low-cost tourist accommodations and facilities)

	Retail Price	Code		Retail Price	Code
☐ Berlin on $40 1992–93	$12.00	D002	☐ Madrid on $50 1992–93	$13.00	D014
☐ Copenhagen on $50 1992–93	$12.00	D003	☐ Paris on $45 1992–93	$12.00	D018
☐ London on $45 1992–93	$12.00	D013	☐ Stockholm on $50 1992–93	$13.00	D022

FROMMER'S WALKING TOURS
(With routes and detailed maps, these companion guides point out the places and pleasures that make a city unique)

	Retail Price	Code		Retail Price	Code
☐ Berlin	$12.00	W100	☐ Paris	$12.00	W103
☐ London	$12.00	W101	☐ San Francisco	$12.00	W104
☐ New York	$12.00	W102	☐ Washington, D.C.	$12.00	W105

FROMMER'S TOURING GUIDES
(Color-illustrated guides that include walking tours, cultural and historic sights, and practical information)

	Retail Price	Code		Retail Price	Code
☐ Amsterdam	$11.00	T001	☐ New York	$11.00	T008
☐ Barcelona	$14.00	T015	☐ Rome	$11.00	T010
☐ Brazil	$11.00	T003	☐ Scotland	$10.00	T011
☐ Florence	$ 9.00	T005	☐ Sicily	$15.00	T017
☐ Hong Kong/Singapore/ Macau	$11.00	T006	☐ Thailand	$13.00	T012
☐ Kenya	$14.00	T018	☐ Tokyo	$15.00	T016
☐ London	$13.00	T007	☐ Venice	$ 9.00	T014

FROMMER'S FAMILY GUIDES

	Retail Price	Code		Retail Price	Code
☐ California with Kids	$18.00	F100	☐ San Francisco with Kids	$17.00	F004
☐ Los Angeles with Kids	$17.00	F002	☐ Washington, D.C. with Kids	$17.00	F005
☐ New York City with Kids	$18.00	F003			

FROMMER'S CITY GUIDES
(Pocket-size guides to sightseeing and tourist accommodations and facilities in all price ranges)

	Retail Price	Code		Retail Price	Code
☐ Amsterdam 1993–94	$13.00	S110	☐ Miami 1993–94	$13.00	S118
☐ Athens 1993–94	$13.00	S114	☐ Minneapolis/St. Paul 1993–94	$13.00	S119
☐ Atlanta 1993–94	$13.00	S112	☐ Montreal/Quebec City 1993–94	$13.00	S125
☐ Atlantic City/Cape May 1993–94	$13.00	S130	☐ New Orleans 1993–94	$13.00	S103
☐ Bangkok 1992–93	$13.00	S005	☐ New York 1993	$13.00	S120
☐ Barcelona/Majorca/ Minorca/Ibiza 1993–94	$13.00	S115	☐ Orlando 1993	$13.00	S101
☐ Berlin 1993–94	$13.00	S116	☐ Paris 1993–94	$13.00	S109
☐ Boston 1993–94	$13.00	S117	☐ Philadelphia 1993–94	$13.00	S113
☐ Cancun/Cozumel/ Yucatan 1991–92	$ 9.00	S010	☐ Rio 1991–92	$ 9.00	S029
☐ Chicago 1993–94	$13.00	S122	☐ Rome 1993–94	$13.00	S111
☐ Denver/Boulder/ Colorado Springs 1993–94	$13.00	S131	☐ Salt Lake City 1991–92	$ 9.00	S031
☐ Dublin 1993–94	$13.00	S128	☐ San Diego 1993–94	$13.00	S107
☐ Hawaii 1992	$12.00	S014	☐ San Francisco 1993	$13.00	S104
☐ Hong Kong 1992–93	$12.00	S015	☐ Santa Fe/Taos/ Albuquerque 1993–94	$13.00	S108
☐ Honolulu/Oahu 1993	$13.00	S106	☐ Seattle/Portland 1992–93	$12.00	S035
☐ Las Vegas 1993–94	$13.00	S121	☐ St. Louis/Kansas City 1993–94	$13.00	S127
☐ Lisbon/Madrid/Costa del Sol 1991–92	$ 9.00	S017	☐ Sydney 1993–94	$13.00	S129
☐ London 1993	$13.00	S100	☐ Tampa/St. Petersburg 1993–94	$13.00	S105
☐ Los Angeles 1993–94	$13.00	S123	☐ Tokyo 1992–93	$13.00	S039
☐ Madrid/Costa del Sol 1993–94	$13.00	S124	☐ Toronto 1993–94	$13.00	S126
☐ Mexico City/Acapulco 1991–92	$ 9.00	S020	☐ Vancouver/Victoria 1990–91	$ 8.00	S041
			☐ Washington, D.C. 1993	$13.00	S102

Other Titles Available at Membership Prices
SPECIAL EDITIONS

	Retail Price	Code		Retail Price	Code
☐ Bed & Breakfast North America	$15.00	P002	☐ National Park Guide 1993	$15.00	P101
☐ Bed & Breakfast Southwest	$16.00	P100	☐ Where to Stay U.S.A.	$15.00	P102
☐ Caribbean Hideaways	$16.00	P005			
☐ Marilyn Wood's Wonderful Weekends (within a 250-mile radius of NYC)	$12.00	P017			

GAULT MILLAU'S "BEST OF" GUIDES
(The only guides that distinguish the truly superlative from the merely overrated)

	Retail Price	Code		Retail Price	Code
☐ Chicago	$16.00	G002	☐ New England	$16.00	G010
☐ Florida	$17.00	G003	☐ New Orleans	$17.00	G011
☐ France	$17.00	G004	☐ New York	$17.00	G012
☐ Germany	$18.00	G018	☐ Paris	$17.00	G013
☐ Hawaii	$17.00	G006	☐ San Francisco	$17.00	G014
☐ Hong Kong	$17.00	G007	☐ Thailand	$18.00	G019
☐ London	$17.00	G009	☐ Toronto	$17.00	G020
☐ Los Angeles	$17.00	G005	☐ Washington, D.C.	$17.00	G017

THE REAL GUIDES
(Opinionated, politically aware guides for youthful budget-minded travelers)

	Retail Price	Code		Retail Price	Code
☐ Able to Travel	$20.00	R112	☐ Italy	$18.00	R125
☐ Amsterdam	$13.00	R100	☐ Kenya	$12.95	R015
☐ Barcelona	$13.00	R101	☐ Mexico	$11.95	R016
☐ Belgium/Holland/Luxembourg	$16.00	R031	☐ Morocco	$14.00	R017
☐ Berlin	$13.00	R123	☐ Nepal	$14.00	R018
☐ Brazil	$13.95	R003	☐ New York	$13.00	R019
☐ California & the West Coast	$17.00	R121	☐ Paris	$13.00	R020
☐ Canada	$15.00	R103	☐ Peru	$12.95	R021
☐ Czech and Slovak Republics	$15.00	R124	☐ Poland	$13.95	R022
☐ Egypt	$19.00	R105	☐ Portugal	$16.00	R126
☐ Europe	$18.00	R122	☐ Prague	$15.00	R113
☐ Florida	$14.00	R006	☐ San Francisco & the Bay Area	$11.95	R024
☐ France	$18.00	R106	☐ Scandinavia	$14.95	R025
☐ Germany	$18.00	R107	☐ Spain	$16.00	R026
☐ Greece	$18.00	R108	☐ Thailand	$17.00	R119
☐ Guatemala/Belize	$14.00	R010	☐ Tunisia	$17.00	R115
☐ Hong Kong/Macau	$11.95	R011	☐ Turkey	$13.95	R027
☐ Hungary	$14.95	R118	☐ U.S.A.	$18.00	R117
☐ Ireland	$17.00	R120	☐ Venice	$11.95	R028
			☐ Women Travel	$12.95	R029
			☐ Yugoslavia	$12.95	R030